TALES OF A LANDLOCKED SAILOR

Joseph E. Crowley

December 21, 2006

Laplacian Press
Cambria, California

Copyright ©2006 Joseph E. Crowley.
All rights reserved.

Publisher's Cataloging in Publication Data

Tales of a Landlocked Sailor
Includes 18 illustrations
1. Memoirs
I. Title II. Crowley, Joseph E. 1911 -
ISBN 1-885540-20-5

Although the stories told here are believed to be true, the names of persons, places, and organizations have been changed to protect their privacy.

Published by Laplacian Press
A Division of Electrostatic Applications
PO Box 896
Cambria, California 93428, USA
email: electro@electrostatic.com
web: www.electrostatic.com

Printed in the United States of America

To Mary,

with all my love

Contents

Prologue	9

Rocky Gap

Grandma Noble and the Molly Maguires	12
Street Smarts Are Not New	15
Katie Killane	16
The Firefighters of Rocky Gap	18
The Night the Lights Went Out in Rocky Gap	22
Me and Bobby MacCree	23
The Story of Shamus McMoore	25

Germantown

Germantown	30
A Very Merry Christmas	31
Ready or Not	32
The Theater District	33
Near Disaster at the Punk	37
The Theater District II	38

The 30s

Manayunk	42
The Depression	43
A Real Bargain	45
Almost Missed Mass in Latrobe	46
911—1933 Style	47
The Power of Prayer	48

World War II

Yes They Can	52
There's One Born Every Minute	53
Boston and Beyond	56
Where Ignorance is Bliss	58
The Manger	60
A Friend in Need	61
Dave, the Captain and My Car	63
In Denial	64
When in Maine, Do As	66
A Matter at Shield's	69
Heil Hitler	71
Not a Poster Sailor	73
Ted DeLorme	75

Raising a Family

Advice to New Parents	78
The Great Lampshade Mystery	79
A Ride on the Merry-Go-Round in Sea Isle	80
The Beheading	81
The Television Set	82
No Ask, No Tell	83
The Christmas Scene	84
Haute Cuisine	85

The Navy Yard

Same Name	88
Harry's Party	90
Commodore John Barry	92
They Wanted Their Report Back	94
Bargaining with Bankers	96

Unions

Devil and Imps	98
The Italian Union Leaders	99
Them Bells	101
Joe Gahagen v. George Meany	103
Remember Me?	105
How High the Moon	108
The Electrician	110
Sometimes Too Good Is Bad	112

Government

Connally and the Admirals	116
The Best Laid Plans	117
It All Depends	120
McNamara's Band	121
Rugged Individuals	123

Teaching

The Story of Seymour Gould	128
My Colleague	130
Me and an Indian	131
A Shooting at the Top of the River	132
Chinn Ho and I	133
A Police Escort in Detroit	135
Me and Melvin Belli	136
Mary, the TV Critic	137

Retirement Travels

Surprise	140
Follow the Leader in Cork	142
A Tale from Trieste	143
You're in My Seat	144
A Pride Of Lions	145
Me and Kit	146
Earthquakes And Us	148

8

Epilogue: Times Change
(A Note to Our Grandchildren) **151**

Prologue

I've heard it said that when an old person dies, a little bit of history dies with him or her. I suppose that's true; so in order to save the little bit of history that I experienced, I'm telling these stories.

This is by no means the story of my life. It is just a recounting of the things I've done, or seen, or heard, or was told over a long period of time. A period of time, in fact, when more changes occurred than in any other era in history: Inventions—radio, television, and computers to name a few; the field of medicine; air travel; destruction or radical changes in century-old institutions; destruction of old values with nothing to replace them. A vacuum being filled with new and strange ideas espoused by people of the worst stripe, and accepted by a great number of people who should know better. And then there were the Wars. World War I, World War II, Korea, and Viet Nam, not to mention all the little conflicts all over the world. And don't forget the Great Depression. A very interesting time. And if the old Chinese curse "may you live in interesting times" ever came true, it did for me.

You won't find here any recriminations and, I hope, any whining. There are no stories about my failures, or about being vilified and rejected, or about being treated unfairly or about those who treated me badly. All of these happened; but I'm trying to follow President John F. Kennedy's advice, "Forgive your enemies, but remember their names."

I'm also emulating an elderly gentleman named Uncle Mose. One Sunday in a Baptist Church in Central Georgia, the minister was exhorting the congregation to forgive their enemies and thus turn them into friends. To emphasize his point he said, "Take Uncle Mose sitting here in the front row. Uncle Mose is ninety-five years old, and I'm certain he hasn't an enemy in this world." Uncle Mose replied, "You're right, Reverend. All those bastards that did me dirt died a long time ago."

In many of my stories I appear to be the hero. That's because I was; and also because it's not only the winners who write the history. The survivors also do.

As I look back on a long and eventful life, I remember what

someone said about "A Tale of Two Cities[1]." He said he wouldn't read anything written by a guy who couldn't make up his mind.

But Dickens was right. Every age has good times and bad times coexisting with a minimum of friction. Evil exists with good (remember the biblical enemy who sowed weeds with the wheat?), poverty with richness, sadness with joy, success with failure, love with hatred, danger with safety, piety with sin—and I've experienced them all. So even in the evil of war there is the good of kindness.

If these stories give you a sense of what it was like for one person to live through most of the twentieth century, then I have succeeded.

---

[1] which starts, "It was the best of times, it was the worst of times"

Rocky Gap

Grandma Noble and the Molly Maguires

Like so many other immigrants, my Grandfather, John Noble, came to America without his family.

Back home in Birmingham, England, his wife Mary—née Draught—and their two children, James and Mary, waited for him to send for them. It was a two year wait.

John settled in Rocky Gap, Pennsylvania and got a job with the Coal Company as a miner. He had learned his trade in England.

After two years, John had saved enough money to send for his wife and children. The mail between Rocky Gap and Birmingham left a lot to be desired in those days, and perhaps even now. Somehow, John and Mary decided on the details of the move from England to Rocky Gap. They picked the date, the ship, and the destination, and John prepared for the arrival of his family. He had rented a "company house" on the "Far Side" and was getting it ready. John planned to meet his family in Philadelphia on a certain date and take them to the Gap by train from the Reading Terminal.

Unfortunately, the transportation was no more dependable than the communications, and Mary arrived in Philadelphia a week before she was due. She knew no one in Philadelphia, and her fellow passengers had their own problems. There were no phones or faxes and no way she could reach John.

Stuck in a foreign city with two small children and no one to help her, she decided to go to the Gap. Finding her way to the Reading Terminal, leading Mary and James, and carrying her baggage, she boarded the train for Rocky Gap. She must have been a remarkable woman.

Meanwhile, John, who was expecting her a week later, was putting the finishing touches on their new home, completely unaware that his family was nearing the Gap.

The express trains did not stop at Rocky Gap. Instead they passed that town and stopped at Sugar Springs Junction five miles down the track. The ride from Philadelphia to the Junction left much to be desired when I rode it, many years after my Grandmother did. I can imagine what it must have been like back in the 1860's for a woman from another country, on her own, with two children and a mound of luggage, riding in a dirty, smoky rail car to a place she had never seen, and not knowing what to do when she got there.

The ride to Sugar Springs Junction must have taken six or seven hours. When I knew it many years later, the Junction had a small, unattractive station where passengers getting off the main line train waited for a small train—later a bus—to take them to Sugar Springs.

The main line train continued to Harleytown, leaving my Grandmother with her children and baggage in a very lonely place. I suppose someone told her how she could get to Rocky Gap—by walking five miles down the railroad track.

She had just about loaded herself up when a large man appeared out of the darkness. He introduced himself and asked who she was and where she was going. She told him her name, said she had just arrived from England and that she was going to her husband—John Noble—in Rocky Gap.

The stranger said he knew John and would give her a hand with her baggage. Together they walked down the tracks; he carrying her bags, and she leading the children. I suppose they talked about her journey and what Rocky Gap was like—things strangers talk about when they share each other's company for a short time.

He led her through the Gap to my Grandfather's house and delivered her, the children and her baggage to my Grandfather. I suppose she thanked the man who had helped her, and I further suppose that he said he was glad to be of help.

When my Grandfather got over his surprise at the early arrival of his family, they had a real reunion. Then he asked her if she knew who brought her from the Junction to the Gap. Of course, she said she didn't know who the kind stranger was, but he said his name was Pat Hester. My Grandfather told her Pat Hester was the Head of the local Chapter of the Molly Maguires. That meant nothing to my Grandmother. It meant lot to some other people.

The Molly Maguires was an organization of Irish miners founded to protect themselves from the most severe exploitation by the mine owners and managers. Back then, Irish Catholics were treated with scorn and hatred, and subjected to the most inhumane and dangerous working conditions. There were no government agencies to help them, so they decided to help themselves. The Molly Maguires seemed an appropriate response to the treatment the Irish Catholic received. It's interesting to note that the people who caused the conditions that led to the formation of the Molly Maguires are rarely criticized.

One man's terrorist is another man's freedom fighter. Saints or sinners—take your choice.

Some years after he walked my Grandmother home, Pat Hester and several other Molly Maguires were tried, found guilty of murder, and hanged in Pottsville. That's where the story ends for most people.

In truth, Milton Shapp, Governor of Pennsylvania in the 1960's, pardoned all of the Molly Maguires who were hanged, including Pat Hester. He found that their trial was illegal and a farce, tainted by bigotry and manufactured evidence. I knew the lawyer who secured the pardons—John Elliott, originally from Shenandoah, Pennsylvania.

I never saw my Grandmother, but I often wonder what she thought of Pat Hester. I remember seeing my Grandfather once. He was a small white figure on a very clean white bed, just about to die. I wonder, too, what he thought of Pat Hester.

I did know Pat's great-grandson. He was a good and old friend of mine.

Street Smarts Are Not New

My Father told me this story.

A long time ago in Ireland, when it was under British rule, a bag of money fell off a Royal Mail coach as it was passing through a village where Jamie Cronin, a thirty-year-old retarded man lived. He found it and brought it home to his mother.

When she saw what it was, she told her son that it was about time he began his education. He was not enthused, but he was an obedient son and he agreed.

So the next day she took him to the school and enrolled him. When he came home after school, he told his mother that he didn't want to go back—saying the kids laughed at him and teased him and made him cry. She said she understood, and that he didn't have to go back.

About two weeks later two detectives came to the village to see if anyone there knew anything about the lost money bag. No one knew a thing about it until they asked Jamie. He told them he found a bag and gave it to his mother. Then they interviewed Mrs. Cronin.

She said she didn't remember Jamie giving her any bag and that there must be some mistake. She asked Jamie when he gave her the bag and he replied, "You remember, Mom. It was the day before I started school." She looked at the detectives and shrugged with compassion.

They thanked her for her time and left.

Katie Killane

When many Irish immigrants came to this Country, they brought with them not only their Catholic faith but also certain other beliefs and customs. I heard about some of them, but it was difficult to get anyone to talk about them.

One I remember mandated that a man—not a woman—should be the first to enter a house after midnight on the first day of the new year.

Another detailed the greeting one should make upon entering a room where there was more than one person. One should say, "God bless all here" or "Hello everybody" or a similar all-inclusive greeting. Naming the people in the room could lead to omitting someone and that person would suffer dire consequences if that happened. This was called "the overlooks."

Another was called "Praying Prayers." Believing that vengeance was the Lord's (and not the injured person's), praying prayers was an appeal to Him to right a wrong. Stated another way, it was a crime that cried to Heaven for vengeance.

And that brings us to Katie Killane. Katie was an elderly gray haired woman with an angelic face, a soft voice, and a gentle manner. She was our cousin, but I'm not sure if that means she was a blood relative. Among the Irish of those days, kinship was based on a number of factors in addition to blood. Where one came from in Ireland, who was in a certain group, who was in the same parish, who had the same friends or enemies—all these were almost as important as blood in determining kinship—or "friendshaft."

Long before I met her—when she was younger—she had had a dispute with a banker over money. Katie was sure the banker had cheated her; he insisted he had not. When it became clear that the dispute could not be settled, Katie said to him, "You're walking on me now but within a year, I'll walk on you." I doubt that the banker was impressed.

About nine months later, the banker, a young man who had always been in good health, suddenly became ill. The doctors could not diagnose the disease, let alone treat it. In a week he was dead, and the cause of death was never determined.

Katie went to the funeral and to the cemetery. She lingered after the mourners left and waited patiently for the grave to be filled in. When it was, and the gravediggers had left, Katie walked on the grave.

The Firefighters of Rocky Gap

Fortunately, there were few fires in Rocky Gap.

If there had been more, the place would have disappeared long ago, not so much from the flames alone, but from the flames aided and abetted by the volunteer Fire Company.

The Rocky Gap Volunteer Fire Company had almost everything. It had a very comfortable Firehouse with a well stocked bar, two pool tables, several dart boards, a full pantry, a modern kitchen, a furnished dining area, a jukebox, a radio, and a large lounging area with comfortable sofas and chairs and several card tables. There was even a small sleeping room with four bunk beds for emergency use—like getting too drunk to make it home. With all of these things, there was barely enough room for the engine.

And what an engine it was. The pumper, as it was called, was a combination machine with pumps, long and short ladders, hoses, and everything needed to fight a fire in a small town. It was the pride and joy of the Company.

The house was indeed not only a firehouse but also a social center for its members, surpassing by far any other social facility in town. And its members were envied.

The Company had picnics once a month in the summer; it had dances once a month and a busy calendar of other social events. It was an active organization with a long waiting list of applicants. And it had a Ladies Auxiliary whose members were in charge of the "fund raisers," the cooking, and the social affairs. It was an ideal place for the elect to hang out twenty-four hours a day. Being an emergency organization, the Firehouse was always open for the members.

To some degree, it was also the social arbitrator of the Gap. Membership was granted only after a searching inquiry into the applicant's background, and a slip or a lapse from the Company's standard was the kiss of death. To put it another way, if any member didn't like you, you were blackballed. On the other hand, if you were just like the members by any standard, you were in. And membership gave you status and your own key. No wonder it was highly prized.

As I said, the Fire Company had nearly everything. The only thing it didn't have was anyone who knew anything about fighting fires.

But it successfully competed with other fire companies in the region and had a number of trophies to prove it. Once a year, all the companies of the region got together and vied with each other in certain events. The winners were given trophies, and I remember seeing some of them in our Firehouse. Best Barbecue Sauce, Best Uniform, Best Decorated Engine, and Best Ladies Auxiliary are a few I remember, and I'm sure all of them were well deserved.

There wasn't any training activity that I was aware of. I suppose the members felt that, since there were so few fires, training to fight them would be a waste of time. After all, who joined to fight fires?

But I do remember seeing our brave lads fight a few fires. A memorable experience!

It was about seven o'clock one summer evening when the breeze blew Mrs. Shannon's curtains into the flame of her stove and set the kitchen afire. Her husband tried to put it out while she ran to the Firehouse for help.

Fortunately, several members were at the bar, and, as soon as they finished their drinks, they donned their coats, boots, and helmets, and ran to the pumper. The driver couldn't start it since there was no gas in the tank. Recriminations flew among them, but the member responsible for gassing the pumper was never found. The driver siphoned some gas from his own car, started the pumper, and, with sirens screaming, away they went.

As they approached the burning house, they slowed down. Two men jumped off the back of the pumper, holding the hose, which they attached to a water hydrant. The truck proceeded slowly as the hose played out. I'm sure the firefighters must have seen the maneuver somewhere, but they were probably not paying full attention to how it was done.

As the truck moved slowly toward the fire, the hose became taut. Suddenly, one end of the hose pulled the hydrant out of the ground, while the other end pulled the pump off its base. It was quite a sight. Water gushed from the ground where the hydrant had been as the pump was pulled from the truck. Then the pumper ran out of gas.

The crowd greeted these developments with a mixture of astonishment and glee, while the firemen stood around with open mouths. Then the crowd started calling names—none complimentary, most of them extremely insulting. Those nearest the gusher were the most uncomplimentary. The Chief, when he recovered, asked who was the stupid bastard who connected the hose to the pump. He received no answer. He didn't know that the pumper should have stopped before the hose ran out.

In the meantime, a neighbor sprayed his garden hose on the fire and put it out. His action went largely unnoticed by the firemen and the crowd, who had more important things on their minds.

The firemen were trying to think of a way to get the truck back to the house, now that it had run out of gas again. They ended up by using a car to tow it home. The crowd, now soaking wet, was seeking a way to cap the geyser. They finally stuffed the outlet with rags while seeking the cut-off valve. They eventually found it, two miles away.

A few radicals were for burning down the Firehouse and everyone in it, but wiser heads prevailed and decided that ridicule was more effective. Our brave lads were referred to after this in the most unflattering terms. The names they were called, if nothing else, showed the originality and wit of the citizens. It became so bad that our brave lads stopped going into the many bars in town and confined their drinking to the bar in the Firehouse, where they could blame each other for the fiasco without any kibitzing by outsiders. The ladies in the Auxiliary did not escape unscathed. They were accused, perhaps unfairly, of cooking meals that caused idiocy in those who ate them. In fairness, it should be said that most of the unkind remarks came from people who were denied membership.

The second, and only other, fire where I saw our boys in action was also in a house.

The fire here started in a bedroom, and careless smoking was blamed. Our boys arrived and, ignoring the flames on the second floor, began to smash in windows on the first floor. I never understood the purpose of this maneuver.

While they were engaged in this pastime, the lone occupant of the house escaped from the bedroom to the roof of an attached shed about five feet from the ground. He was ignored by the firefighters, who were busy breaking windows, and he started to scream for help.

The crowd looked on impassively while he screamed. Finally someone said, "Jump down, y' Lug, you're only five feet from the ground." Apparently, this means of escape hadn't occurred to the fire victim. When he digested the suggestion, he jumped with no ill effects.

His escape went unnoticed by our brave lads, who were now on ladders, breaking windows on the second floor. Eventually, they turned their hoses on the fire, put it out, and poured so much water into the room that the second floor collapsed onto the first floor, which in turn collapsed into the basement.

The firefighters congratulated each other on their achievement.

They had successfully turned a very minor blaze into a total disaster. The owner of the house didn't share their enthusiasm and threatened to destroy the Firehouse and the Engine to prevent our boys from going to any more fires. He never did. But his threat had an effect. Other citizens joined his cause and the message to our brave lads was loud and clear—"Go to another fire, and we'll burn down the House and the pumper."

Shortly after that the Rocky Gap Volunteer Fire Company became officially an "Inactive Company." It retained all the rights and privileges it previously had. It just didn't go to any fires.

When the Company was declared "Inactive," the members continued their routine: getting drunk, hosting barbecues, competing with other companies, having dances and picnics; and, in general, having a ball. The members kept the pumper polished but were not interested in its running condition. After all, it was driven only once a year to the Convention of Fire Companies. I heard it won third place in the best-polished engine competition there.

In short, the members did the things they were good at, and avoided those things beyond their expertise, like fighting fires. And every one was happy.

Some said the Fire Company was the best fire prevention program in history. Just the thought of the Company being revived was enough to frighten grown men. Who in their right minds would want our brave lads to screech up to their house and destroy it in the name of saving it? So everyone became very conscious of the danger of fire and did everything, including praying, to assure that their homes were fireproof.

As a result of their efforts, there hasn't been a fire in the Gap for many, many years.

The Night the Lights Went Out in Rocky Gap

About eight o'clock on a Wednesday evening, the lights went out in Rocky Gap; the lights on the streets, in the bars, in the stores, in the churches and in every house, except one. The Pennsylvania Power and Light Company, which supplied electricity to the Coal Region, had suffered a severe power outage.

When the people rushed out to the street, the only thing they could see was Jim Malloy's house shining like a beacon in a sea of darkness. It was an eerie sight. Naturally, this brought a number of questions, none of which was easily answered.

But, like a jigsaw puzzle, the pieces fell into place, driven by logic. The mine had its own electric generating station. Jim was a mine electrician with knowledge of, and access to, all things electric. Ergo, Jim hooked his house up to the mine's power lines and enjoyed free electricity.

How long this would have continued if the PP&L Co. hadn't suffered it's misfortune is anybody's guess. But there was no doubt about how long Jim would continue as a mine electrician. Just as long as it took management to fire him.

Me and Bobby MacCree

The stillness of a soft summer evening in Rocky Gap was shattered by the sounds of gunshots. Bob MacCree had killed his wife Mary.

Bob MacCree and Mary O'Malley were married in St. Luke's Church after a long courtship. They had known each other since grade school, and everyone who knew them took it for granted that someday they would marry. Everyone, that is, except Bridget O'Malley, Mary's mother. She hated Bob and did all she could to discourage the marriage. She didn't succeed.

Both Bob and Mary were popular, and their marriage was thought to be perfect. Their friends said it was a match made in heaven.

After the wedding, the couple moved into their own home and set up housekeeping. Bob was a hard working miner and Mary—as they said—kept a "clean house." Both of them were always willing to help a neighbor, and everyone liked them. They seemed devoted to each other, and the only cloud on their horizon was Mary's frequent and long visits to her mother who lived a short distance away.

The visits became more frequent, and Bob often found his wife at her mother's when he came home from work. Bob was a patient husband, and, apart from his complaining about the time she spent with her mother, they seemed to get along well.

As Mary's visits to her mother became longer and more frequent, and as Bob's frustration grew, they started to quarrel. Whether her mother, who hated Bob, urged her on, or whether Mary had enough of the quarreling, she moved out of their home and back to her mother's house within a year of their marriage.

Bob had asked Mary to return home every day since she moved out, but she refused, and her mother told Bob not to come to her house again.

On the evening of the shooting, Bob went to the O'Malley house and asked his wife to come out on the porch. She came as far as the doorway. Her mother stood behind her, screaming at Bob, and told him Mary was staying with her.

Bob pulled a handgun from under his shirt and shot his wife

three times through the heart. Some said he should have shot his mother-in-law, but that's a matter of opinion.

As soon as the shots were heard, the whole town came to life. People ran out of their houses and out of the bars, all asking what had happened. When the word of the shooting spread, most of the town hurried to the O'Malley house. Father O'Neill, who was one of the first to arrive, gave Mary the last rites, and a couple of mine safetymen tried to resuscitate her; but it was too late. Doctor Conway pronounced her dead at the scene, and someone called the State Police.

The first trooper arrived in about fifteen minutes, and three more screeched up shortly after. When they learned what had happened, two policemen started looking for Bob. They found him at his house, as if waiting for them.

Bob was indicted, tried, and found guilty of manslaughter. He was sentenced to twenty years in prison, and released after serving twelve.

Many years later, I was taking the early train from the Gap to Philadelphia. My Uncle Tom walked me to the station, which was deserted except for one man. My Uncle introduced us and suggested that, since we were both going to Philadelphia, we would be company for each other.

He was a pleasant and interesting man, and we talked about many things—the kind of things two strangers talk about while sharing each other's company for a short time. When we reached the Reading Terminal, we said goodbye and went our separate ways.

About six months later, I was in the Gap again, and my Uncle asked me what I thought of my traveling companion on my last trip to Philadelphia. I said he was a pleasant and interesting man who made a long and boring journey pass quickly.

Then he reminded me of the killing of Mary MacCree, and it all came back to me—including her husband's name. I couldn't believe that the man who rode to Philadelphia with me was the same man who killed his wife.

As far as I or anyone else knew, Bob MacCree had never broken another law and was respected as an upright citizen.

This was the first time I met a killer.

The Story of Shamus McMoore

It's been a long time since I first met Shamus McMoore.

I was on an errand for my Aunt, who wanted me to deliver a package to a friend of hers in the upper part of Rocky Gap. As I walked through the "Patch" a young boy of about eight greeted me, "Hi Butt, you don't have a drink on you, do you?" I told him I didn't, and he followed up by asking me if I had a cigarette I could spare. I told him I didn't, and, if I had, I wouldn't give it to him since he was too young to drink or smoke. He told me what I could do with myself, and, when I moved toward him, he took off like a rabbit and disappeared around the corner of a house.

When I got home, I told my cousin Bill of my meeting, and he said I must have run into Shamus McMoore. He filled me in on the history of Shamus.

This young man was the oldest son of a widow with four other children who was struggling to survive. The only help she received was from neighbors who didn't have much more than she did. She just didn't have the time or the energy to supervise Shamus, who was on his own since he was five. He was always in trouble, but no one wanted to take any action against him because of his mother. So he went from bad to worse, was expelled from school countless times and always taken back for another chance because of sympathy for his mother.

I saw Shamus a few times after my encounter with him but never up close. We just didn't travel in the same circles. But I did hear stories about him from time to time; most of them unbelievable although the tellers always swore they were true.

Pat Hurley, a friend of mine from the Gap, told me the most unbelievable story when I ran into him in Washington, DC during the War.

As Pat told it, Shamus went to Harleytown the day after Pearl Harbor to enlist in the Army. Somehow he was accepted, given a cursory physical exam, sworn in and shipped to Indiantown Gap for processing.

During processing, he was given a thorough physical. When his blood was being examined, the doctors found that there was some kind of an antibody which, when extracted and powdered, was a miracle coagulant. My friend was unclear on what this was and admitted that he may have gotten it wrong. But he was sure that Shamus' blood was rare and the Army wanted it badly.

So Shamus was transferred to Walter Reed Army Hospital in Washington and was assigned a menial job—which he never did—and was available to give blood whenever the doctors wanted it. He was treated like a prized cow, pampered and cared for. But that didn't change Shamus one bit.

He continued his wicked ways, getting drunk, fighting, and in general causing hell wherever he went. The Army had a problem. After one particularly bad drunk, in which Shamus picked on the wrong guy and was badly beaten up, the Army solved its problem. Shamus' blood was too important to be wasted in a fight—after all, it was the Army's blood, and it meant to keep it.

So a team of six MP's were assigned to guard Shamus twenty-four hours a day. At least two of them went with him everywhere. In particularly rough situations all six guarded him. They watched him in the hospital, when he was on the base, when he went on the town, when he went on leave, and when he was asleep. Their sole order was, "Don't let anyone touch Shamus." And they followed that order.

My friend Pat had some first hand experience with Shamus and his companions.

The way he told it, Shamus was given two weeks leave, and he and his guards headed for the Gap. Shamus slept at home, and the six MP's were put up in three houses near his mother's. Two of them were with him at all times. The other four were probably writing letters asking for transfer to a war zone.

Shamus continued his life style. He arose about four o'clock in the afternoon, much to the disgust of his mother. After a leisurely bath he got dressed, had his breakfast, and was ready for a night of carousing. Accompanied by his guards, he visited his first saloon. He started to drink and soon was insulting the few patrons who were drinking that early. When one of them got up to give him what he deserved, Shamus ducked behind one of his guards while the other confronted the attacker and stopped him from getting anywhere near Shamus. Our boy watched this with amusement, taunting the attacker and daring him to fight.

One of the MP's led Shamus out of the bar while the other restrained the patrons. But before he left, Private McMoore threw a glass of beer at the bartender.

This performance was repeated in every bar in town every night of Shamus' leave. After a week of this, the whole Gap was ready to join the German Army just for the chance to kill Shamus.

But the MP's did their job so well that Shamus finished his leave unscathed. That can't be said for the MP's. As they put it, they didn't join up to babysit a no-good drunk. In fact, one of them said he was ready to kill not only Shamus but also the officer who assigned him this duty.

According to Pat, the Gap breathed a sigh of relief when Shamus went back to Washington.

Shamus never came home again, and no one knew what happened to him. The more religious members of the community attributed his disappearance to the novenas they made; others were sure that someone had killed the little bastard. No one really knew or cared. They just wanted Shamus never to come home again. As far as I know he never did.

Germantown

Germantown

There are no walls in Germantown.

The Rich,
    the Poor,
        the In-Betweens
live together in Germantown.

But there are walls in Germantown.

A Very Merry Christmas

(as told by Mary)

During World War I, the government urged everyone to become at least partially self-sufficient by having a Victory Garden. That was all the encouragement my Father needed.

We were living in Fox Chase at the time, and we had enough ground to plant a garden. So he went to the General Store near our home and stocked up on tools, seeds, fertilizer and all the other necessities for a rather large garden. While he was at it, he also bought fifty chickens, which he thought would give us enough eggs to feed a family of ten.

At that time, my Father was a Superintendent at Cramps Shipyard and often had to work two shifts. This gave him little time to tend his Victory Garden, and when he tried to enlist my mother in the effort, she reminded him that she was a "city girl" and knew nothing about gardening.

It wasn't long before reality set in, and my Father concluded that a Shipyard Superintendent would not be a successful Victory Gardener.

So, right before Christmas he returned the tools and what was left of his other purchases to the General Store. The manager took them back with one provision—No cash; but my Father could exchange them for other goods.

The General Store had everything, including toys and dolls. So my Father loaded up on sleds and bikes for my brothers, dresses and books for my older sister, and I got the largest and best doll I ever had.

It was a very Merry Christmas.

Unfortunately, the chickens could not be returned, and we had chicken dinners for a long time.

Ready or Not

(as told by Mary)

After my Grandmother died, my Grandfather, their three single daughters, and my Grandmother's brother, Uncle Dick, lived together. When Uncle Dick died, they left the house they had lived in for many years and moved into an apartment.

As my Grandfather got older his activities became more limited, and finally he was confined to bed. His daughters gave him excellent care, did everything for him, and sheltered him from the problems of life. In all probability, it was this care that prolonged his life. Finally, his health deteriorated, and his daughters decided that he would appreciate the consolation of religion. They asked a local minister if he would visit my grandfather.

The minister readily agreed and when he saw my Grandfather his first question was, "Mr. O'Connor, are you prepared to meet your Maker?" My Grandfather replied without hesitation, "I don't know. You'll have to ask the girls."

There is no record if the minister asked the girls or, if he did, what the girls replied. But it does show how well the girls did their job.

A few weeks later my Grandfather did meet his Maker, and I'm sure he was as well prepared as anyone could be.

The Theater District

I never heard anyone compare Germantown with Broadway, but we had our movie houses and we patronized them regularly.

Our Theater District stretched up Germantown Avenue from Manheim Street to Chelten Avenue, with a jut to the right at Armat Street and a jut to the left at Chelten. There were other theaters outside this area, but we never considered them as part of our turf and never went to them.

When I was a pre-teen and early teenager, the theater of choice of our set was the one at Germantown Avenue and Manheim Street. It had many names over the years—one time it was the Manheim, then the New Lyric—but no matter what official name it had, it was affectionately known to us as "The Punk." The origin of, and reason for, the name are lost in the mists of antiquity.

For us the Punk had three major attractions: it was the closest one, it screened the type of movies we liked, and it was the cheapest. Ten cents got you any seat in the house.

The Punk was home to the Saturday Afternoon Serial and action movies of all types, with Westerns predominating. It was the place to be on Saturday afternoon, and the Saturday Matinee was the highlight of the week. To us, it was not only a movie house but also a social center where we met friends, discussed the latest happenings, and made plans for the future. With about two hundred kids shouting at the top of their lungs, it was a noisy place.

It was de rigeur to be outside the Punk at least forty-five minutes before the doors opened. It was then we met our friends, decided who would sit with whom, whom we would avoid, what we would do after the movie and, most important, where we would sit in the house. It was this latter decision that led to the most conflict since everyone had a "best seat," and, all too often, that seat was also the "best seat" of a number of other kids.

The accepted tactic was to have the fastest runner in the group get closest to the door. When it opened, he could rush in, reserve a row of seats for his group, and wave wildly to show his position. Sometimes it worked; sometimes it didn't. And if your group lost, there was always a verbal assault on the winners who responded in kind but maintained their position. By the time the argument was over, all the "next best seats" were taken, and the losers had to scramble to get any seat all. As a result the group was split and scattered, and their unity and cohesion was put to the test. After all, who could enjoy the show separated from one's friends?

Once inside, the patrons continued their conversations, and the separated brethren screamed at each other across the aisles, but it wasn't the same as sitting near your friends.

There was a rigid code of conduct for the patrons. Girls were segregated from boys. The girls sat in the last several rows on the right hand side as you came in. No boy should ever sit with a girl unless ordered by his mother to sit with his sister. This edict resulted in the boy saying to anyone who would listen, "She's my sister." The sister never said a word. She just looked straight ahead and ignored her brother. What she told her mother when she got home is another matter.

Everyone had to leave his seat at least four times during the show. Everyone had to talk to friends in other rows during the performance.

Every romantic scene was to be booed with the oft-repeated warning, "Don't nobody look." Some of the more sophisticated patrons would loudly announce that they were taking a nap and requested that they be awakened "when it's over."

"Talking Pictures" were far in the future when the Punk was at its prime. The dialog and scene setting were flashed on the screen by subtitles, but something else was needed to set the mood. That need was met at the Punk by a piano and someone to play it.

The piano was a beat-up upright, and the player was a heavy blond. When she marched down the aisle with both arms filled with music, smiling at the patrons, it was a changed place. The conversations stopped, everyone settled into their seats, and the anticipation could be felt in the air. She arranged her music, the lights dimmed, she struck an opening chord, and the screen lighted with the promises of things to come. They were called "trailers."

The Blonde could play that piano. The music was scored to match the action on the screen, whether it be a wild chase or a tender love scene. Of course there were times when it was hard to hear the music with all that was going on in the audience. As a concession to public safety, and in a vain attempt to appear upscale, the Punk had an usher. These individuals—and there was a new one every month or so—were interchangeable. They all needed a shave and wore badly fitting uniforms, including caps that were either too big or too small. I suspect that management bought one uniform and firmly believed that "one size fits all." The ushers all had one thing in common—they were smart enough never to go into the audience. Instead they stood in the back and blew a whistle when the noise became unbearable.

There was no such word as interactive in those days, but that's what it was. The patrons reacted to everything on the screen, usually in a loud voice; advising the actors, warning them, and, in most cases, critiquing their performances in clear and specific terms.

Disagreements on these matters among the patrons were usually settled by screaming matches, with the loudest screamer winning. By that time, the surrounding patrons were screaming at the screamers to shut up, and the theater went back to its usual steady roar. Many questions about what happened while the disagreement was being settled were asked by those who missed the show on the screen while participating in the show on the floor.

A kiss on the screen was the prelude to chaos. Screams, threats, protest marches, and vows never to come to this movie house again were common. To add to the confusion, some of the patrons who left their seats to participate in the protest had difficulty in reclaiming them. Either they forgot where they sitting, or their seats were occupied by other patrons. By the time these problems were solved—some never were—the movie had moved on from the kiss, and the ever present question, "What happened?" was asked a hundred times.

Not surprisingly, there were no protests when the hero kissed his horse.

After a couple of hours, the show was over. The lights came on, the Blonde gathered up her music and wisely waited until most of the audience had departed. Remaining were those who had lost their hats and coats. They mounted a search which would have done credit to a police evidence squad. In most cases, the hats and coats were found—but not always. The management told the losers that they could come back later to see if their possessions were found, and this caused an outcry. The big question was, "What am I going to tell my Mother?"

As we trooped out through the lobby, we discussed our plans for the next Saturday, which, in retrospect, were just like the plans for all the preceding Saturdays.

When we were out of the theater, reality returned with a bang, and we suddenly were thrust out of the world of the silver screen and into the real world, which was not nearly as exciting or glamorous.

But we took some of what we saw with us; the names of the movies—"The Perils of Pauline" and "The Hooded Terror" were two—and the names of the stars—Tom Mix and Hoot Gibson come to mind. In fact, if the picture was particularly impressive, we played the roles back in the neighborhood.

I can still remember the hero who lived inside a mountain cave. When he approached his hidden cave, a part of the mountain was lifted, and he rode in. Just like our modern-day garage door with its opener. Once inside, he could see who was approaching his cave very easily. A bell would ring, a light on a numbered grid would go, he would look through a periscope-like instrument, and he would see who the intruder was. Just like the security cameras we have today.

Maybe our old heroes were smarter than we thought.

During the week, the Punk was another theater. Its matinees were sparsely attended, but the evening shows on certain nights were something else. In an effort to boost attendance, many theaters gave away glassware and china on certain nights. This program appealed to the ladies, and they quickly became addicted to all those free glasses, plates, cups, and saucers. They never missed a "glass night" if at all possible, and proudly displayed their treasure in their china closets.

They never thought that their finds would be highly prized many years later as "depression glass." Too bad we didn't save ours.

Near Disaster at the Punk

One Saturday, there was a near disaster at the Punk.

When the kids arrived about twelve for the one o'clock show, they were greeted by a line of pickets carrying signs proclaiming to the world that the New Lyric was unfair to organized labor. We didn't know what that meant, but the word spread fast in our working class neighborhood, and soon the fathers arrived to see what it was all about. They told us to go across the street so that we wouldn't be accused of crossing a picket line. That would be a disgrace we would never live down.

The manager was out front, screaming that he was not unfair to organized labor, and the picket captain kept repeating that he had his orders.

Out of this discourse an issue emerged. The Punk had a movie projectionist. The manager said the projectionist was a union member in good standing. The projectionist agreed with the manager. The picket captain said he had his orders to picket the New Lyric.

Finally a parent (and a staunch union man) suggested that the captain call the Union headquarters and explain the situation. He did, and came out saying that a mistake had been made. He was supposed to picket the Lyric Theater in South Philadelphia, not the New Lyric in Germantown. He blamed the whole thing on a "failure of communication..."

He then told his pickets to get back into their cars, told the manager there was no hard feelings, told the crowd that the Punk was not unfair to organized labor and was not involved in a labor dispute. Then the pickets drove off and headed toward the Lyric Theater.

The parents told the kids it was OK to go into the Punk, and we all rushed across the street. We didn't understand—or care—what was going on. The only thing we knew was that now we wouldn't miss an episode of our serial.

The show was delayed an hour but that didn't upset us since the manager said we would see the whole show.

The Theater District II

As we grew older, our tastes changed. No longer was the Saturday Afternoon Serial the center of our social life. Our vista had broadened and we discovered that Hollywood made other movies, and that these appealed to our changing tastes. These movies were rarely, if ever, shown at the Punk. So we went where they were shown.

One of these theaters was the Germantown. At the Germantown there were no screaming kids, there were no Serials, the seats were cushioned, and the aisles were carpeted. And it had no piano—it had an organ and an organist! It was definitely a step up from the Punk.

While the movies shown there were the big attraction, close to, or maybe even ahead of, the movies was the organist, Karl Bonawitz, who made the Blonde look like a first year piano student. Of course the organ was a big help since it had several keyboards, numerous pedals and all the sound effects you could imagine. Every instrument was represented, from flutes to bass drums, and when Karl started to play and added those "special effects," it was out of this world.

There was no question about Karl's musical ability. He was at the top of his profession. In fact, he was the organist at the dedication of St. Francis of Assisi Church in Germantown in 1928 and received rave notices.

There was a question about Karl, raised by my female relatives and their female friends, which was of no interest to me or my male relatives and friends. The question was, "Does Karl Bonawitz wear a corset or does he not?" When my Aunt or Cousin took me to the Germantown, I heard this question debated endlessly, and the debate continued at home with no decision ever being made.

The Germantown showed better pictures with better actors and actresses, and it was there that we saw "Ben Hur" and similar epics, as well as the more modest ones like "Abie's Irish Rose."

A half block up Germantown Avenue was the Colonial Theater. It was much larger than the Germantown and had a balcony and Peanut Gallery. It also had a larger organ, but the organist was no

Karl Bonawitz.

It was a real competitor to the Germantown since it screened similar pictures. I can remember seeing "The Public Enemy" with James Cagney there.

If you went up Germantown Avenue and turned left on Chelten Avenue, you would soon come to the Orpheum, a massive theater which not only showed movies but was also a vaudeville house. This was the Queen of the Theater District. Its prices matched its show—25 cents to a dollar depending where you sat. For a while, a friend of ours was a security guard there, and we were often his guests.

Finally, there was the "Bandbox" on Armat Street. It had the reputation of being avant-garde. For us, that was the kiss of death. We believed that it was patronized by "half cuts[2]," and we wanted nothing to do with them. Bad as this was, it was nothing compared to the rumor that it screened foreign films with English subtitles. That did it. I doubt if I went there more than three times.

All of these theaters have long ago disappeared—torn down, remodeled into stores or just abandoned. While physically gone, they live in the memory of their former patrons who still survive.

---

[2] social climbers, snobs

The 30s

)ebaters Win Twice From Vill
ake First Place In Intercollegiat

DEBATER

Joseph E. Crowley

Manayunk

The Hills are steep in Manayunk.
    Going up is hard and slow in Manayunk.
    Going down is fast and easy in Manayunk.
Life is like the hills in Manayunk.

The Depression

I can still remember the beginning of the Great Depression of 1929.

My Father was just beginning his work at LaSalle College, and I heard on the radio that banks were closing, including the bank that held his money, and that the depositors in all likelihood would loose everything they had in the bank. I hurried to LaSalle, and found my Father eating lunch with his workers. I told him the news and said the radio broadcast said that the depositors were out of luck. He took the news in silence, and, when I asked him what he was going to do, he told me that he didn't see that there was anything he could do right then. And he continued eating.

Bank after bank failed; the stock market was devastated; people lost their jobs and their homes; and many who on paper had been quite well-off found themselves penniless overnight. Many found that the situation was just too much to bear and killed themselves. Others tried to sell their possessions just to survive—if they could find buyers. Anyone who had cash could find bargains all over the place.

Factories closed, companies folded, and people tried everything they could think of just to survive. Former executives turned to doing odd jobs if they could find any, while many turned to "junking" to keep alive. "Junking" was picking through trash to find something that could be sold.

As the depression continued year after year, a number of programs—private and governmental—were instituted to help the unemployed. Soup kitchens and breadlines were common, and the "Apple" program was born. Under this, you could buy apples from the government at a very low price, sell them for a higher price, and make yourself a profit. Nearly every busy corner had at least one "apple seller" open for business. No one became rich selling apples.

It's probably a good thing Roosevelt was elected. If the do-nothing of Hoover continued, in all probability, there would have been a revolution.

Once Roosevelt was in office, program after program came out of Washington, each one trying to solve a specific part of the general problem. We had the PWA[3], the WPA[4], the General Relief Program and many others. Some worked well, some didn't; but all offered some hope— which was in short supply—as well as immediate help.

---

[3] Public Works Association
[4] Works Progress Administration

A Real Bargain

If nothing else, John Whitehead was a real bargain hunter. He would travel miles to save a buck, and if he heard of a sale he was off and running.

One time, he went shopping on South Street in Philadelphia and bought two dozen of men's socks for fifty cents. South Street was about a two-hour trolley ride from Germantown, but time or distance meant nothing to John when a bargain was to be had.

I happened to be in his house when John unveiled his bargain. He had two dozen socks all right, but there was a slight problem. None of them matched. If two were of the same color, they were different sizes and, if they were the same size, they were different colors.

When he saw what he had bought, he flew into a rage and called the South Street merchants every unpleasant name he could think of. He grabbed the socks and dashed out, screaming that he would show those bastards what would happen to them for cheating him.

During the ride from Germantown to South Street, John's anger grew. It was at a boiling point when he saw the merchant who had cheated him. He grabbed him by the throat and was well on the way to strangling him when the police arrived and pulled John off his quarry.

They put him in the patrol car and drove away. They made it to 11th and Market and told John to take the 23 trolley to Germantown and never come back to South Street.

As far as I know, he never did.

Almost Missed Mass in Latrobe

It was a long time ago—back in 1933—when the LaSalle football team traveled to Latrobe, PA to play St. Francis. I was the manager, and with my assistants we handled all the details of the trip.

We won the game and did a little celebrating on Saturday night, but not much.

Frank Connelly, the Pennsylvania Railroad representative, traveled with us and arranged to have the Pittsburgh-Philadelphia Express make a stop in Latrobe to pick us up. We had two private cars for our party, as we usually did when we traveled. The train was to stop for us at six in the morning.

We checked the Mass schedule at the local church, and the first Mass was at five AM, so we decided we could make it.

All the Catholics on the team, together with the coaches, the fans and the managers, were at the Mass at five o'clock. The priest preached an overlong sermon, and we began to get edgy. Finally at the last Gospel, about ten minutes to six, we all walked out. As we reached the door, the priest yelled at us, "You haven't heard Mass." We kept on going and met the train as it was pulling into the station. We were on our way home, not believing that we missed Mass.

I understand things are slightly different today.

911—1933 Style

(as told by Mary)

Back in 1933, there was no 911 but we managed to handle emergencies in our own way.

I was riding the street car down Fifth Street going from the office to my District to teach the clients the best ways to use the food they were given.

The ride was uneventful for the first ten minutes, and then the motorman stopped the car and announced that anyone who wanted to get off before Palmer Street should do so now since he was making no stops before reaching Saint Mary's Hospital. It seemed that one of the passengers was going into labor and had to reach the Hospital as soon as possible

A few people left the car, the motorman pushed the controller to the limit, and away we went down Frankford Avenue with the bell clanging all the time. We raced through cross streets, warning cars and wagons to get out of the way, until at last we screeched to a stop at Saint Mary's.

The motorman helped the pregnant passenger into the Hospital and shortly returned to the car. He was treated as a hero by the waiting passengers and, after saying, "It was nothing," continued the journey down to Market Street.

911 couldn't do it better, and probably not as well.

The Power of Prayer

I graduated from LaSalle College in June, 1934 and found that a job in the Federal Government I had been promised disappeared when my sponsor, for some reason unknown to me, was removed from his job.

So I joined the ranks of the unemployed and started looking for work. The only thing I could get was a position with the high sounding title of Assistant Registrar at LaSalle. The salary was indefinite—which was whatever LaSalle could afford, and that was about a couple of dollars a day.

Every Monday, Eddie O'Neill, who was going to Temple and working as a beer truck driver, came to my office, and together we walked to the Miraculous Medal Novena on Chelten Avenue, hoping for the best.

There we attended the Novena along with thousands of others, each asking the Blessed Mother to intercede for us to get whatever we were praying for. The Novena was the most popular religious ceremony, and every session—there were about twenty a day—was overflowing.

We never told each other what our hope was, but we were sure that it had to do with some material thing.

After about six weeks, Eddie told me that he had received what he had been praying for—a new pair of shoes!

He was living with his Aunt and Uncle at the time—Ella and Frank Smith.

Ella had bought Frank a pair of shoes, and, when Frank tried them on, they were too small. Ella asked Eddie his size, and, '"Behold!," it was the same as the new shoes. So rather than returning them, Ella gave them to Eddie. His prayers were answered.

I had to wait a little longer.

In August of that year, the State of Pennsylvania announced that it had one hundred jobs in the Relief Agencies, which were to be filled by the end of the year. Only those with a college degree were eligible to apply. I applied, and, together with a hundred thousand other college graduates through the State, took the exams. I was one of the lucky ones, and in December, 1934, I became a Visitor for the Philadelphia Relief Board and was assigned to the Germantown Office. My salary was $18.75 a week. At that time, a fortune.

World War II

Yes, They Can

At the beginning of World War II, I was a manager of the War Manpower Commission in Philadelphia and, among other duties, was responsible for promoting the hiring of women in industry. What a job!

Since only men were hired to do industrial work, the employers that I spoke to thought that I had rocks in my head and told me so in many ways. I spoke of the coming shortage of men in the labor force. I spoke of the large pool of available and trainable women. I spoke of all the assistance available to employers who hired women. Nothing I said made any impression. Men worked, and women stayed home.

In one meeting with employers, where I was exhorting them to hire women, I said, "There's no job a man is doing that a woman can't do." From the back row came a voice, "Sure there is—female impersonator!" What a put-down! "Victor/Victoria" was far in the future.

As the War went on and men were drafted, my role changed from an appealer to an allotter. Now I was besieged by the same employers who had thought I was nuts, asking for all the women they could hire.

There's One Born Every Minute

Shortly after World War II began, the pressure on the War Manpower Commission to staff the war machine increased at an alarming rate. New approaches to recruiting and allocation were tried every week. One of the more successful was inviting representatives of the employers with authority to hire into our buildings and directing applicants to them. It worked very well, and we were able to match workers and jobs much more efficiently.

Many employers took advantage of our offer, and we usually had twenty to forty employers in our buildings at any time. Getting in was easy. We screened applications from employers and conducted various checks to make sure they were legitimate before we let them in. Or we tried to.

One day a very impressive black man came in and asked to participate in our program. He identified himself as Frederick M. Raley and said that he represented the Millwright Company in Ohio, which was expanding to fulfill a government contract that had just been given the Company. The new plant was just about finished, and the Company was ready to hire new employees.

All of this was confirmed by a letter from the president of the Company stating Mr. Raley was authorized to hire 100 workers and transport them to the Company's housing project, which had just been completed. They and their families would move in, and report for work the day after they arrived. The rent would be ten dollars a month, and their transportation would cost them nothing. There was just one thing. The Company wanted to hire only black workers since the Board of Directors wanted people of color to participate fully in the war effort.

That was all right with us since there was no law prohibiting it, and black workers were hard to place in Philadelphia. So we told him he could start as soon as we finished the paperwork. He knew what we would do.

We had a standard checking procedure and, when we put him through it, he came out smelling like a rose. We were told in writing by the Company that he was authorized to hire applicants, that it had been awarded government contracts, and it was seeking 100 new employees. The letter confirmed the transportation and housing arrangements. Sounded good.

On Monday morning, we gave him space in our Center City Office and he was in business.

He had advertised in the black papers, and especially in the Tribune—the largest in town, and his ads were like manna from heaven to the black community—good jobs for which they would be trained if necessary; good wages; and good new low-cost housing.

We were deluged as soon as the ads appeared, and soon we had to give the recruiter more space. In two weeks, he had more than his hundred new employees.

On his last day, he thanked us for letting him use our facilities and gave us a letter from the president of his company thanking us profusely for our help.

The recruiter told us his special train would leave the Reading Terminal at 8:00 PM Sunday night and would take the newly hired men and their families to their houses in Ohio. He stressed that they must be in the Reading Terminal by 6:00 PM. He said he had given each man a folder containing detailed instructions, and he anticipated no difficulties. We congratulated him on his successful recruiting effort, and he went on his way.

About seven o'clock Sunday evening our Manager in Charge of Recruiting received a phone call from the Police Department requesting that someone from the Manpower Commission come to the Reading Terminal immediately to help quash a riot. He rounded up some of his bosses—fortunately I was at Sea Isle City—and they descended on the Terminal. The recruiter had never appeared and had checked out of his hotel.

I was brought up to date on Monday. It was a sorry tale.

When our people arrived at the terminal, they were met by a hundred black men, along with their relatives and friends, all on the verge of mayhem. The police were hard pressed to keep any kind of order, and the railroad officials were screaming at the police to move the mob out of the Terminal.

Out of all this came the following story.

During the interview or after—it was not clear which—the "newly hired employees" were told that Mr. Raley had just received word from the Millwright Company that each of them would be required to give him twenty-five dollars as "good faith" deposit to make sure they would show up at the Terminal. The money would be returned to them when they reached Ohio. Those who couldn't raise that amount could not be hired. Amazingly, a hundred applicants paid him the twenty-five dollars. They were told not to tell anyone about this because the Company had told him to collect one hundred dollars from each applicant. He told each one that he was collecting that amount from everyone but the man he was talking to. Mr. Raley was getting only twenty-five from him because of his work history. But the applicant was sworn to secrecy and was told everyone would be in trouble and no one would be hired if he talked. We never found out if he told the "employees" this tale when he interviewed them or afterward. No one in our office heard that he was asking for money, and none of the "employees" ever said a word about it.

The "employees" started arriving at the Terminal with their families and friends about one o'clock, and by six the place was overflowing. Everyone was looking for Mr. Raley, and the Railroad Officials who were asked about him said they never heard of him. They also said they knew nothing about a special train to take the "employees" to Ohio and asked the Police to remove everyone who didn't have a ticket. What followed was a nightmare.

The men were screaming that Mr. Raley had their tickets; women and children were crying; railroad officials were demanding that everyone leave; and the hapless police and our representatives were trying to maintain law and order. Unsuccessfully, I may add.

By eight PM, it was clear to everyone that Mr. Raley wasn't going to show up. The hotel manager said he checked out late Friday night and left no forwarding address. (The manager found out on Monday that Mr. Raley's check for over a thousand dollars was no good.) Sadly, and with great reluctance, the "employees", their families and friends began to leave the Terminal, shouting that we in the Manpower Commission would pay dearly for what we had done.

The next week was a busy one for us. Our calls to the Millwright Company brought us more grief. We found out that the Millwright Company was not increasing its work force, that it never heard of Mr. Raley, let alone authorizing him to hire a hundred workers, and that it never received any inquiry from us concerning Mr. Raley.

We found out much later that Mr. Raley had a friend in the mailroom of the Millwright Company who also had access to the stationery of the Company, and that was all he needed.

Back in our office we were kept busy explaining that we too were the victims of Mr. Raley, that we did all we could to check him out, and that we were not responsible for this scam. I doubt if any of the "employees" believed us. Eventually the episode was forgotten by all but the victims.

The scam got little, if any, coverage by the mainstream newspapers, but the Tribune played it up big and identified Mr. Raley as "a white con man." So much for objectivity and responsible reporting.

Boston and Beyond

After a short leave when I graduated from Officer Candidate School at Princeton, I went to Boston, got a room at the YMCA, and reported to the First Naval District Headquarters for assigned duty. It was on a Sunday.

The only person around was a grizzled old chief who took my orders, endorsed them, and told me the Headquarters would be open on Monday and I should report to the DCPD[5]. He added that no one was around the Headquarters since this was Sunday. I remembered that, centuries ago, the warring factions didn't fight at night, on Sundays, or on Holidays, but I didn't know the custom was carried over to the present day. Later on I learned that sacrifices were sweet only when needed.

On Monday, I reported to the DCPD's office at seven AM, but no one was there. I waited, and at eight-fifteen some civilian clerks arrived and at about eight-thirty the officers started arriving. Then Commander Ted DeLorme put in his appearance.

The Commander was a tall, thin man and very friendly. He asked me about my background and said he understood I was an executive with the War Manpower Commission in Philadelphia in civilian life and remarked that I was just the kind of an officer he needed, He said he wanted to introduce me to the other members of his staff and he would talk to me later.

I met Fred Land, who had the same kind of assignment in Rhode Island, and Leo Carney, who did the same thing in Massachusetts. Fred was from the War Manpower Commission in Mississippi and Leo from the Commission in Erie, Pennsylvania. The three of us were to become the closest of friends.

The Executive Officer was Lt. Commander Koch, who handled the day-to-day operations of the Office, assisted by several other officers, Walt Seamen and Dick Buschman. One other officer was later accused of being a Communist agent, court-martialed, and convicted. We didn't talk about him, but we knew he came from a prominent Boston family and that his father was a professor at

---

[5]District Civilian Personnel Director

Harvard.

After lunch at the Officers Club in the Boston Shipyard, the commander called me into his office and told me that I was to represent the Undersecretary in Maine, New Hampshire and Vermont. He said I would be the Navy member on the War Manpower Commission, the War Production Board, and the Selective Service Board for each State and that I was to make certain that Navy contractors were to receive whatever men and material they needed.

I asked him where my office in Portland would be, and he said that was up to me. He said that since I used to be a Manpower Commission official, I should see if the Manpower office in Portland would let me work there. I told him I heard that the Navy had installations all over Portland, and maybe I should work in one of them. He told me that under no circumstances should I stay in any Navy office and that I was not under any Navy Command except his Office and the Undersecretary. When I was directed by him, I would represent the Commandant of the First Naval District. In other words, I was on detached duty, answering to no one but him. I hadn't learned about that at Princeton either.

He asked me where I was staying, and I told him at the YMCA and asked him when I should leave for Portland. He looked at his watch and told me there was a train leaving Boston at four o'clock, and, if I hurried, I could make it. It was then a quarter to two. He wished me luck, gave me a letter, and told me to keep in touch. He also told me to come to Boston for a meeting on the first Saturday of each month. I said good-bye to my new friends, but, before I left, the Lt. Commander told me to call him when I was settled in Portland.

I rushed to the YMCA, gathered my clothes, paid my bill, rushed back to the North Station, and just made the train to Portland. I read the letter when I got settled on the train, and, to my surprise, it said that I was the Field Representative of the Undersecretary of the Navy, and all Naval Personnel were to give me any and all assistance necessary to carry out my duties. It was signed by an Admiral Breckworth, who was identified as Chief of Staff for the Undersecretary of the Navy. It was to come in handy.

Thus began my Navy career, and I was to learn what "detached duty" was.

Where Ignorance is Bliss

When Commander Ted DeLorme said goodbye to me and sent me to Portland, he told me to visit the Bath Shipbuilding Company in Bath, Maine and see Pete Newell, who owned the Company and was its president. He said to let Pete know I was in Maine, to tell him I represented the Undersecretary, and I was there to help him in any way I could. I didn't consider this a high priority since I had more important things to do. Like getting an office, and finding a place for Mary and the kids to live.

After I was settled and had taken care of some urgent business, I remembered what Ted had told and called Newell for an appointment. I identified myself, and he said he'd be glad to meet me. We agreed on a date later in the week.

I got one of my cars and drove up to Bath, was admitted to the Yard and directed to Newell's office.

On the way, I noticed a sign over an office reading, "U.S. Navy Superintendent of Shipbuilding." I learned many things when I was at Princeton but nothing about Superintendents of Shipbuilding, and I wondered what he did. I thought it would be proper to visit another Navy Office; so I went in, asked to see the Superintendent, and was taken to his office. Captain Joyce was a reserved gentleman. He said he was glad to see me and asked if he could help me in any way. I thanked him for the offer, and said I'd let him know if I needed help.

He asked what office I was associated with, and I told him I was the Undersecretary's field representative. He looked at his Assistant, Commander Hitchcock. He asked if I came to see him, and I told him that I had an appointment to see Mr. Newell and that's why I was in Bath. The Captain and the Commander looked at each other but said nothing. I said that I had to leave to see Mr. Newell, and the Captain said that the Commander would go with me to Newell's office. I told him that I didn't want to impose on either of them and I could find my way there.

I had a pleasant visit with Mr. Newell who said that he appreciated my coming to see him and that he would welcome me back at any time. He was a typical Mainiac,[6] pleasant but reserved, and I liked him.

I drove back to Portland without stopping at the Supship's Office, and, although I saw Newell, the Captain, and the Commander many times afterward, this incident faded from my mind.

About 14 years after this incident I met Hitchcock—now a Captain and married to Newell's daughter—at the First Naval District Headquarters in Boston. He told me a story I found hard to believe.

About three weeks before I arrived for my conference with Newell, a civilian consultant to the Navy was meeting with the Captain and the Commander at their Bath Office. During his stay, a destroyer built by Bath was being turned over to the Navy, and, of course, a formal dinner celebrated it. The consultant said he'd like to go and asked the Captain to arrange it. The Captain said he was a guest himself, but he'd see what he could do.

He managed to wrangle a ticket for the consultant, but it was for a table in the far back of the room. When the Captain gave it to him, he said he was insulted and that he should have a seat at the head table. Joyce told him he should be glad he had any seat, and, if he were smart, he'd take his ticket and sit at the table to which he was assigned. The consultant took his seat but made it clear that the Captain was not one of his favorite people. The consultant's name was Struve Hensel.

When I left the Supship's office, the Captain called the Commander and told him he better pack his bag because the Captain was packing his. The Commander said he didn't understand. The Captain asked if he remembered the name of that obnoxious civilian who raised a fuss over his seat at the dinner. "Yes, it was Hensel." Do you know who was recently appointed Undersecretary of the Navy? "Yes, it's Struve Hensel." Next question: Who does that young Lieutenant work for, and what's he doing here talking to Pete Newell? Answer: "Oh my God!"

According to Hitchcock, the two of them were on edge for several months waiting for the axe to fall. But it never did.

I explained that I knew nothing about it and my visit to Pete Newell was purely routine. Hitchcock said that if they had known that, they wouldn't have had to go through several unpleasant months.

Moral: Don't jump to conclusions.

---

[6]person from Maine

The Manger

On the first Saturday of each month, we Field Representatives went to the Headquarters in Boston to attend the DCPD[7] meeting. We reported on our activities, the problems we ran into, how they were solved, and what we anticipated in the months to come. All the other Department Heads reported on their work, and the whole idea was to keep everybody informed. The meetings started at eight, broke for lunch, resumed, and broke at three so Leo, Fred, and I could catch our trains. We were the envy of the other officers since we were on detached duty, while they were under the eye of the DCPD.

The week before our first meeting, the three of us agreed to meet for dinner at the Officers' Club and then get our rooms. We met as planned, and, after dinner, we bought four bottles of liquor at the club and set out to find a place to sleep. The Hotel nearest to the Headquarters was the Manger, and we decided to stay there.

We went to the hotel and waited our turn, hearing most of those in line in front of us being told no rooms were available. When our turn came, the three of us went to the desk as one and placed on the counter three bottles of booze each wrapped in paper. The Desk Clerk was an older Irishman and, as soon as we announced our names, he said our reservations had been received and our rooms were ready for us. This didn't sit too well with the people who had been turned down, but who said life is fair?

We followed this procedure as long as we had our meetings, and we were always assured of rooms when rooms were hard to get.

I went back to the Manger years later when I had business in Boston, but it had fallen on hard times and was just a shell of what it used to be. The Desk Clerk had long since departed; for a better place, I hope.

---

[7]District Civilian Personnel Director

A Friend in Need

When I had to go to the northern part of Maine, I usually stayed in the BOQ[8] at the Dow Army Air Corps Field outside of Bangor, Maine. The people there were very hospitable, and I was given a room with privileges at the Officers' Club and PX[9]. Over time I got to know some of the Officers rather well and made some real friends. Incidentally, it was in the Officers' Club that I first heard of the death of President Roosevelt. Not everyone was saddened by the news.

One night about nine o'clock, I received a phone call at home from one of my friends—a Lieutenant at Bangor. Somehow he had tracked me down and was rather upset.

It seems that he was in charge of a fifty-truck convoy going from Boston to Dow Field and somehow miscalculated the amount of gas needed. When the convoy got to Portland, it was obvious they had to be gassed up, so he to went the Naval Station and asked for gas. He was turned down flat.

He told the people that he would replace the gas as soon as he got to Dow, but they still said, "No", explaining they were running low themselves. He asked me if I could help him out. I got his phone number and said I'd call him right back.

I finally got my friend Dave at his home, explained the situation to him, and asked what he could do to help me. Dave asked only one question, "Is this guy a friend of yours?" I told him he was, and Dave said, "Tell him to drive the trucks to our tank farm and I'll meet him there in twenty minutes."

I called the Lieutenant back, gave him the directions to the tank farm, and told him to meet Dave there in twenty minutes with the trucks.

About an hour and a half later, the Lieutenant called me, thanked me and said how much he appreciated my help. Dave then got on the phone and said everything was taken care of. I thanked him and told him I would see him the next morning. The

---

[8]Bachelor Officers' Quarters
[9]Post Exchange (store)

following day I saw Dave, thanked him and gave him a bottle of Irish whiskey—his favorite.

Dave was a civilian who really ran the motor pool and everything connected with it. I asked him what happened last night and he told me. The Lieutenant contacted the Commander who was in charge of all transportation on the Base and the Commander, who didn't like the Army Air Corps because of some past slight, saw his chance to get even and took it. I asked Dave if he would get on the Commander's list for helping out. He said the Commander wouldn't know about it, and, if he found out, Dave would tell him the Undersecretary's representative OK-ed the deal and that would scare him off.

I was back in northern Maine a few weeks later and asked if I could stay at the BOQ. I was told I could, but first the Commanding General would like to talk with me. I was escorted to the General's Office where he told me how much he appreciated what I did about the gas and I was welcome on the Base at anytime. He told his Aide to put me in the Visiting Generals Suite and asked me to have breakfast with him the next morning. The suite was fine, the breakfast was great, and from then on I was a VIP at Dow. Even when the War was over, I thought I was in the airline business. But that's another story.

Dave, the Captain and My Car

One morning, I went to pick up my car for a trip to Augusta. As I approached the Transportation Office, I heard and saw Dave in a heated conversation with a captain. Heated on the captain's part; Dave was his usual calm self.

It seems that the captain, who had just arrived in port, wanted a car for the day, and Dave was insisting he had no cars available. The captain wasn't going to take "No" for an answer and insisted that Dave find him a car. Dave said he had none.

I waited outside the Office and, when there was a break in the captain's tirade, Dave said to me, "Your car will be right up, Lieutenant." With that, the captain went ballistic and ended his tirade by screaming at Dave, "Give me that lousy Lieutenant's car!"

Dave kept his cool and replied, "That lousy Lieutenant, as you called him, happens to be the Field Representative of the Undersecretary of the Navy and, if you want his car, you take it away from him, but don't expect me to do it."

Just about then, a driver brought my car up and held the door open for me. I thanked the driver, thanked Dave, saluted the captain, got in my car, and drove off. I could hear the captain screaming as I drove out of the garage.

Apparently, no one told him that life is not fair.

I wondered what he would say if he knew I had another car in the garage.

In Denial

When I was in Maine during the War, I did a lot of traveling, carrying out my duties. Once, I stopped in a small town overnight on my way to Fort Kent, in the far reaches of the state, right on the Canadian border.

The town had been a resort in peacetime but was now a real backwater. It had a large hotel, but all of it was closed except a small wing which accommodated a few permanent guests. I had no trouble getting a room, and the owner—who was also the desk clerk—told me that the dining room was featuring a lobster dinner that night and that I was welcome to eat there. I quickly accepted the invitation. The meal was delightful. There were seven of us at the one table: the owner and his wife, a man in his fifties, a girl in her twenties and a middle-aged couple. All of them were permanent guests in the hotel.

I could sense that they were wondering what a Naval Officer was doing in that part of Maine, far removed from any water. But as Maine people, they were too polite to ask. There were comments such as, "We don't see many Navy people up here" and, "Is that Navy car out front yours? Any news about those German spies they were supposed to have caught near Calais?" I finally said that I was on my way to Fort Kent to help a contractor who was having labor problems.

From the looks they gave me and each other, I knew they didn't believe a word I said. I was sure that they gave me a much more romantic or venturesome role. They pictured me as a spy chaser, or carrying out some secret mission they would read about some day, or on my way to a conference where important war plans would be made. In their minds, labor relations was just a cover story. I'm sure I gave them something to talk about for weeks.

After dinner, we went to a large cabin-like room with a roaring fireplace and comfortable chairs. We were joined by a husband and wife who worked as a cook and handyman. I was sure that each had his special chair, and I waited to to be told which would be mine. The host pointed to a chair and asked me to sit.

For the next couple of hours, we had a great time. They told stories of local people and events, always putting them in the best light. When necessary for me to understand what they were talking about, they clued me in.

About nine o'clock, the young lady said it was time for her to leave, and said goodnight to us all. After she had gone, the host said to no one in particular, "That's a shame about her." I knew better than to ask, so I just raised my eyebrows. In Maine, that was enough.

He said that she had married shortly before the War, and, right after Pearl Harbor, her husband enlisted in the Marines. She agreed with what he did.

From the time of his enlistment, she wrote to him every day, and he answered when he could. Then, a couple of years before my visit, she received the dreaded telegram from the Navy Department telling her that he was missing in action after a battle on one of those islands in the South Pacific.

She refused to accept the fact that he was dead, stating that the telegram didn't say that and that the Navy was not above making mistakes. She explained away the fact that she never heard from him by saying that there was a war and he was fighting in some far away place.

So she continued to write to him every night as she had always done. A few letters were returned stating addressee was unknown but most were not.

Before we broke up, the host invited me to breakfast at six the next morning, and I showed up with all my friends. We said goodbye, wished each other luck, and they all said they hoped I would come back and see them. I promised to do it if I could. I never did.

That afternoon, I arrived in Fort Kent, saw the Navy contractor and spent the next couple of days negotiating with people who weren't nearly as nice as my friends in Dover-Foxcroft.

I never found out if her husband came back to her after the War ended. I hope he did.

When in Maine, Do As

One day, I got a phone call from Boston telling me to get to one of our Navy suppliers in central Maine as soon as I could. I said it might be a couple of days since I had several meetings scheduled that week. I was told to postpone them and get to the supplier the next day if at all possible. It sounded like something was up, and, when I asked what it was all about, I was told that this supplier was extremely important to the Navy, and we could afford no interruption to production. They said that was all I needed to know and the problem was a personnel one which I should solve. I was told the supplier would fill me in when I got to the plant.

I postponed my schedule and left for central Maine that day.

I arrived at a small town that evening, found a room, and the next morning asked the host where the XYZ Company was. He gave me directions, and I set off to find it.

It was in an unimposing building right outside of town, and I wondered why the Navy was so interested in this place. I soon found out.

The company was owned and managed by two brothers from New York City and had been in operation for less than a year. It specialized in finely machined metal parts and worked to extremely close tolerances. When the brothers showed me a machine piece, I asked what it was used for. They said they didn't know. The only thing they knew was that the Navy wanted them, and their employees might stop production. It was common for the Government not to disclose the end usage of things it bought if the product was to be used in highly classified programs. I didn't know until after the War that this small piece of metal played a big role in the Manhattan Project.

The brothers explained their problem to me. They had been in business in New York, but came to Maine when they learned that highly qualified machinists were available there. Their recruitment was successful, and they established a good training for those employees who needed to increase their skills. They had about 25 skilled machinists and 20 semi-skilled people. Everything was going fine until the hunting season approached.

In rural Maine—and that is about 98% of it—the men do not work in hunting season until they bag their two deer—one on their license and one on their wife's. This could be a day or two or much longer, depending on their skill and the number of deer available.

The employees told the Company a few days ago not to expect them at work until they bagged their deer limit. This caused a panic attack, and the brother went on a long explanation about the war effort and the need for their product. They intimated that their workers would be unpatriotic if they took time off—the wrong thing to say. From my experience, the Maine people were as a group the most patriotic I ever met. The brothers from New York just didn't know they were in Maine.

So with hunting season less than a month away, I was handed this hot potato.

The first thing I did was to tell the brothers they were not to discuss this statement with their employees. I added that, if they did, I would withdraw from the case, tell the Navy the case couldn't be solved, cancel the brothers' contract, and send the part elsewhere. This was probably shooting an ant with an elephant gun. The brothers were so scared, they would have jumped off a water tower if I told them,

I asked the brothers if the men had any leaders, and they told me that two of the men had first told them about hunting season. I went to the shop floor, introduced myself to the two men, and asked if I could speak with them about the situation. If they agreed, then I would like to meet with all the employees to discuss the problem. Having been in Maine long enough to understand their distrust of outsiders, I told them I didn't want their answer right then but asked them to think it over and let me know their decision. I told them where I was staying.

When I told the brothers what I had done, I thought they were going to cry. Apparently, they thought I would order their workers not to go hunting and not to miss work. I said that, if they didn't like what I was doing, I'd leave, and they could solve this problem themselves. This brought on more moans and an invitation to dinner, which I politely declined.

I was sitting on the porch of the rooming house where I was staying when the two employees came up and sat beside me. We exchanged pleasantries and talked about the weather for a while, when the older one said they thought my offer over and discussed it briefly with some of the men. They were willing to talk. I said, "Fine." Then there was five minutes of silence.

The older one said that they wanted me to know that the men were as interested in getting production out as anyone else. I said I knew that.

He then asked me if I were a hunter. I told him I wasn't, but I thought I knew how important it was to many people in Maine to bag two deer. He asked me if I were from Maine, and I told him I wasn't but my Maine friends had told me about bagging two deer. He asked me what I thought about it, and I said that I thought it was an economic necessity in many cases. Another period of silence.

Then I said I thought the problem was not good against bad, but good against good, and there had to be a way to hunt deer and maintain production too. Another period of silence.

Then I raised some possibilities; but first, we had to get some facts. Like, how many men would go deer hunting? Based on experience, how long would it take to bag two deer? After a long discussion, it looked like we were talking about an average of 2 days.

I made it clear I had not talked to the Brothers about any solution and I was looking for ways to solve the problem. For example, would all the men go hunting at the same time or could it be staggered? Would overtime production make up lost daily production? Would stockpiling production work? I never mentioned not going hunting. I asked the spokesmen to think about the problem, and I would see them the next day. I also said I would talk to the Brothers and get their ideas. I asked if it would be a good idea to meet with everybody when we came up with some ideas. We agreed that it would.

I met with the Brothers the next day to get their ideas, and the only thing they could think of was to fire everyone who didn't show up for work. I asked them if they would get replacements, and they said, "Maybe." I disabused them of that notion quickly, and I explained that the Navy had no authority to order any civilian to do anything, and the Brothers better be careful or they might lose all their workforce. This floored them, and I'm sure they wished they were back in Brooklyn.

Over the next several days, I reached agreement with the spokesmen and presented the solution to the Brothers. They finally agreed, and we all met the workforce after work. The Brothers would get their production and the workers would get their deer. I reported all of this to my superiors in Boston. It worked out well.

A Matter at Shield's

During the War, practically every necessity was rationed. The government issued coupon books to individuals entitling them to purchase rationed goods. The coupons for meat were called "red points." Families usually pooled the members' points to purchase meat. The only meat exempted from "points" was "utility'—the lowest grade of meat, barely edible.

One day a friend of mine, Ernie Reich, who worked for the Manpower Commission, asked me if I could help a friend of his who was in a bit of a jam. I said I would if I could, and he told me this story.

Shield's Supermarket was the biggest and best food store in Portland. We shopped there all the time, and I carried our can of grease there once a week.

Jim Harlow managed the store and one of his employees messed up and sold an agent of the Price Stabilization Board some meat without collecting the proper points. This was considered a very serious crime and could result in a jail term for the responsible people, and withdrawal of verification for the store.

I went with Ernie to talk with Harlow, and he was understandably very upset. He told me what had happened, and it seemed to me that it was simply a mistake by a new employee. I told Harlow that I would talk to someone I knew at OPS[10] and see what I could do.

I saw my friend and told him what I found out about the Shield incident, and that I was convinced it was an error by a new employee and not a pattern. I asked him if perhaps a letter of warning, rather than an official citation, might be appropriate. He called in the investigator who bought the meat, and he said he thought I was probably right.

A few days later Harlow received a letter of warning from OPS telling him to exercise more care in the future and advising him that no further action would be taken by OPS in this case.

Harlow called me as soon as he received the letter, and he was

---
[10] Office of Price Stabilization

on cloud nine. I didn't tell him that my friend from OPS had told me of the decision the day before.

We continued to shop at Shield's and were treated real well.

Heil Hitler

When the War was over, we dropped our service to the Navy contractors like a hot potato. The War Manpower Commission, the War Production Board, and the Selective Service System were all winding down. Those of us who represented the Navy terminated our membership. I remember getting a telegram on the day the War ended telling me I was to spend no more money servicing Navy contractors. We now switched our effort exclusively to the Navy, and we were busier than every.

I was ordered to the Headquarters of the First Naval District in Boston and appointed Civilian Personnel Director. Leo Carney was ordered to Washington, and Fred Land was appointed Personnel Officer of the Separation Center in Boston. All the Field Offices were closed.

Navy personnel by the tens of thousands were streaming into Boston to be separated and, while waiting, they were housed in the Separation Center, which occupied an entire square block in South Boston. Fred was responsible for staffing the Center with civilian employees and keeping all the slots filled. It was an important job, and Fred handled it to perfection.

We lived at the BOQ, and I dropped in to see Fred from time to time. One time, I was in his office when the Catholic Chaplain, Father McMahon, who was a friend of ours, excitedly told us that Hitler's nephew was in his office, and he was going to bring him in to see us.

In a few minutes the Chaplain, accompanied a tall, pleasant-looking young man, came to Fred's office and introduced him. "This is William Hitler, Adolph Hitler's nephew." We shook hands, and Fred asked him if he really was Hitler's nephew. He said he was and was not proud of it. The four of us chatted for about a half hour, with William doing most of the talking. He described his hitch in the Navy but said little about his Uncle.

It seems strange that the nephew of the man who started the war served in the Navy of an opponent, but, after hearing William, it made sense. He disliked his Uncle and wanted nothing to do with him. He said he was delighted that Germany lost the War, and that he was glad to be part of the Navy that defeated him.

He said he didn't know what he would do when he was discharged from the Navy, but he said he was going to look around and see what was opening up. He didn't discuss his immediate family at all.

Father McMahon ended the visit by telling William he wanted him to meet some other friends of his. We said goodbye, and I never saw him again. We checked him out after he left us, and he really was Hitler's nephew.

Not a Poster Sailor

When the War was over I was transferred from Portland to Boston and appointed the District Civilian Personnel Director with a staff of 20 officers and civilians. Now we concentrated on civilian personnel matters in the Navy and had no responsibility for civilians working for Navy contractors.

The Director billet was a captain slot, but I was given it and told that I should perform all the duties assigned. Some of the officers assigned to me outranked me, and all the other department heads were captains. So I had my work cut out for me. The Commandant knew little about civilian personnel and cared even less. He made it clear to me that this area was mine, and that he would depend on me to handle that matter.

More of this later.

Mary and the kids were in Philadelphia, and I shared a two-bed room at the BOQ.

Since the Navy was separating officers and enlisted men at a great rate, the turnover of my room mates was very high. Few stayed more than a week. Many had a story to tell.

One that I remember was told to me by an officer who served in the Pacific as a pilot aboard a baby flattop with no Angel Detail.[11]

Of all the crew, one stood out as the antithesis of a poster sailor. He was lazy, insubordinate, often drunk, and, in short, a real pain in the butt. His name was O'Reilly.

But he did have one redeeming feature.

Because there was no helicopter on this ship, a pilot was pretty much on his own when he went into the drink. And that's where O'Reilly came in.

When a pilot went into the water, O'Reilly—no matter where he was—jumped in the water with a life preserver and swam to the downed plane. He pulled the pilot—many were unconscious—from the plane, put a life jacket on him, and pulled him to the ship. My roommate wasn't sure about how many pilots O'Reilly rescued, but he thought it was more than thirty.

---

[11] A helicopter to rescue downed pilots

Needless to say, the pilots thought O'Reilly was the best thing since ice cream. But, being O'Reilly, he was bound to get into trouble, and almost every week he was at Captain's Mast[12].

But he had his defenders. At every mast, every pilot on the ship appeared as a character witness and urged the captain to inflict no punishment on such a fine sailor. The captain—a former pilot himself—always found a way to mitigate O'Reilly's transgressions, and he was never confined to the brig.

When my roommate left the ship, O'Reilly was still not a poster sailor, was still not in the brig, and was still ready to save any pilot who went down.

---

[12]A naval disciplinary hearing

Ted DeLorme

My first Commanding Officer in the Navy was Commander Ted DeLorme, the father of Rosemary DeLorme, a prominent motion picture actress. About six months after I arrived Ted was relieved by Commander John Craig, and, when I asked where Ted was assigned, I got some vague answer about his being ill.

I never heard from him until some time later, when I was the DCPD.[13] He called me in a very distraught state, asking me to get him out the hospital where he was being held against his will. He was rather incoherent and pleaded with me as an old friend to get him out of the institution where he was being mistreated in a most inhumane manner. I asked him where he was, but before he could tell me, the phone went dead.

I asked the District Medical Officer what the story was with Ted DeLorme. He looked at me in a funny way and asked why I wanted to know. I told him about the phone call from Ted.

He said that Ted had a mental problem, and that's why he was relieved as DCPD. He was transferred to the Psychiatric Ward of the Naval Hospital, where he had been since he was relieved. The MO[14] told me Ted was getting worse, and the prognosis was discouraging. He said he doubted if Ted would ever be released. I asked him if there was anything I could do, and he told me there was nothing. I asked if I could visit Ted, and he told me I wouldn't be permitted to see him.

The Doctor asked me not to say anything about Ted and the phone call—and I haven't until now, when it won't do any harm to anyone.

---

[13] District Civilian Personnel Director
[14] Medical Officer

Raising a Family

Advice to New Parents

We can remember when we were new parents a long time ago. The joy, the wonder, the love, the pride, the apprehension, the nervousness, the uncertainty, the feelings of inadequacy... We remember them all and more. And we share them with all parents, past, present and to come. So it seems fitting that we should pass on to our Grandchildren what we have learned so long ago.

One evening when Joe was about two months old, he didn't seem his usual happy self. He cried, he whimpered, he was restless and we didn't know what was wrong with him. We decided to call the doctor (in those the days you could talk to the doctor and not an answering service), and we knew he would ask if Joe had a fever. So we decided to take his temperature, but we didn't have a thermometer in the house.

I went to the corner drug store, bought a thermometer, and brought it back to the house. When I started to sterilize it, it broke. I went to the store again, bought another one, started to sterilize it, and it too broke. I went to the store again, bought a third, but this time I used a different method of sterilization. This time it didn't break.

We took Joe's temperature, and, to our great relief, it was normal. He stopped crying, smiled and in a few minutes fell asleep. Whatever was bothering him went away, and he was again his happy self. We, too, recovered and were no longer nervous wrecks. We didn't call the doctor.

Now for our advice: Never try to sterilize a glass thermometer by dipping it in boiling water.

The Great Lampshade Mystery

One day when I arrived home from work, I found our five kids kneeling on the living room floor.

I was edified, but before I could say anything, Mary told me that the kneeling was punishment, not piety.

It seems that a person or persons unknown then, and now, had punched a design with a sharp object into Mary's favorite lampshade. The kneeling was an attempt to make the guilty confess or the innocent snitch. The attempt was unsuccessful.

The kneeling stopped for dinner, and then the kids were sent to their rooms to meditate on the evil deed and consider cooperating. That too was unproductive.

The mystery has never been solved...

The lampshade has long since gone, and our kids have long ago established their own homes. Now, whenever they wish, they can punch designs in their own lampshades to their hearts' content.

A Ride on the Merry-Go-Round in Sea Isle

(as told by Mary)

It was one of those cold, miserable evenings in August in Sea Isle, with spitting rain adding to the charm. I decided to take the five kids for a walk on the Boardwalk since they had been in the house all day and were getting a little rammy.

The Boardwalk was deserted. A few shops were open with no customers. At the end of the walk, the Merry-Go-Round was open, with only the owner present.

As we approached, he came out and said we should all come in and have a ride. The kids were all for it and I thought that it was an invitation we couldn't refuse since it would cost us nothing.

So we went in, and the kids had several rides and were having a great time. Then it started to rain hard, and I told the kids we better get home before we would get soaked.

The owner stopped the ride, the kids got off, and we started to leave when the owner said, "That'll be four dollars." I said, "What! You invited us in for a ride and now you want us to pay?" He replied, "I didn't say it was for free."

I paid him two dollars, all I had with me, and decided never to take the kids there again.

Moral: Nothing's free in Sea Isle.

The Beheading

Three-year-olds have their own methods of getting into unusual situations. It's getting out of them that's the problem. We learned that lesson, again, a long time ago when Terry was that age.

One Saturday afternoon, Terry decided that he could put his head in the empty space of a lyre-back chair. He could, and he did. It was when he decided to take his head out of the chair that he had a problem. This he couldn't do, and all his wriggling and screaming didn't help a bit.

The screams brought all six of us running into the living room. When we surveyed the situation, we decided to use the common techniques to release him. We gently moved his head, turning it this way and that to get the best position. Then we rubbed Vaseline on the parts that he couldn't squeeze through. None of these worked, and, after each failure, our kids joined Terry in crying and calling on me to "do something."

Finally, after talking to Mary, I decided to saw the piece of wood which was holding his head. I got a coping saw, and, after assuring Terry that I wouldn't hurt him, I began to saw. This was a prelude to chaos.

As soon as I placed the saw on the wood, Terry began to scream, and the other four kids shouted in unison, "Don't cut his head off!" The crying and shouting did nothing to settle my nerves. Gradually, the saw started through the wood, missing Terry by a comfortable margin. But the screaming continued as I sawed away.

It was at that moment that our oldest friend appeared at the front door. After three years, Eddie O'Neill came to Philadelphia and dropped in on us. We said a quick hello, and he watched as I finished my sawing. Finally, the wood gave way, I eased Terry's head out, the crying and screaming stopped, the tears were dried, and we had a nice long visit with O'Neill.

He later referred to this incident as, "a quiet Saturday afternoon at the Crowleys."

I repaired the chair, and today it is as good as new. Mary and I keep it company. Everyone else involved in the event has gone.

The Television Set

In 1949, we bought our first television set. It was a 10-inch Magnavox in a cabinet with a record player and an AM-FM radio, and we put it in the living room. It was the first one in the neighborhood, and news of its arrival spread quickly among the younger set.

The programming was primitive, and the schedule was limited. I can remember two of the programs. One featured an inept and pathetic pitchman for household utensils who never got anything right. Today it would be called an "infomercial." If he were demonstrating a vegetable peeler, he would cut his hand. If it were a piece of cookware, he would drop it. If it were a hand mixer, he would break it. And so on and on.

Since every broadcast was live—tapes were in the future—his goofs were there for all to see in glorious black and white. But nothing daunted him. He ignored each mistake and moved on to the next disaster. His self confidence, born of ignorance, was something to behold. He was, in short, a fascinating klutz, and I watched him whenever I could.

I'm sure he once worked as a pitchman on the Atlantic City Boardwalk; and I'm equally sure he was fired for incompetence.

The other program I remember was Kukla, Fran and Ollie. This one was a gem, and it entertained millions of kids. Fran looked like a cousin of mine.

Word got out that this program could be seen in our living room and every day when I came home from work, I had to wade through a gathering of kids spread out on the floor. I think the show ran from five o'clock till after six, and it played to a full house at our place.

Fortunately, we had a house at the Shore, so each Summer the show at our house was canceled until we returned in the Fall.

As more and more people got television sets, our audience dropped off until we had none at all. But our guests were not forgotten. Holes remained in our living room rug where some of them had picked off the material while absorbed in the drama on the tube.

No Ask, No Tell

When our kids were in St. Francis of Assisi School, Cardinal Dougherty died. He had been archbishop of Philadelphia for thirty-three years, known to all and feared. That day, the kids came home for lunch and returned to school as usual.

After lunch, Mary turned on the radio and heard the news.

When the kids came home after school she asked Jim if he knew the Cardinal was dead. He said he had heard about the death that morning.

Mary asked him why he didn't tell her, and he replied, "You didn't ask."

Over the years Jim perfected that behavior and now only answers direct questions.

The Christmas Scene

For several years, we painted a Christmas Scene on the plate glass storm window in the front of our home. It was a family affair with lots of suggestions and soon became a tradition.

We finished the scene one year on the Sunday afternoon before Christmas, and that evening Mary and I left for the annual Faculty Christmas Party at LaSalle. Before leaving, we placed the painted window in a secluded place in the front room and warned the kids that the paint was not yet dry and that they should stay away from the window.

When we returned home, we found the window shattered and the painting in pieces on the living room floor. It seems that some of the kids decided to play catch football in the living room, and the passer overestimated the ability of the catcher, or the catcher underestimated the arm of the passer, or both.

In any event, the result was a shattered window.

We repainted the scene on a new storm window, and this time it remained unbroken until January.

Haute Cuisine

Back in the 1950's, a friend of Marys asked her if she would help some French nuns who were on the verge of starvation. It really wasn't that bad, and her friend was exaggerating.

The sisters were members of a French Order that administered a school called Raven Hill Academy, in the upper part of East Falls. Raven Hill was more of a finishing school than a high school and was very exclusive. Many of the students came from other countries—Corazon Acquino, who later became the President of the Philippines, for one—but most were from the States. Grace Kelly—later Princess Grace of Monaco—went there too.

Mary said she would help out if she could and went to the School to see the Mother Superior. She told a sad story.

The House Sister—the only one who could cook—had died suddenly, and there was no one to replace her either locally or from the Order. The sisters tried to cook, but the boarders were close to revolting, and the nuns weren't too pleased either. In those days, there were no organizations like ARA or other caterers. If you didn't cook it, you didn't eat. The Mother begged for help. And she got it.

Mary is a great cook, as anyone who has eaten her meals knows, but she is also a great teacher. After she graduated from Immaculata, she taught Home Economics and helped welfare recipients to manage their households.

So she planned eight sessions of food management from Menu Planning through Purchasing, Preparation, Cooking to Presentation. The classes were conducted on eight successive Saturdays and were attended by two Sisters, one of whom didn't speak English.

At the end of each session, Mary prepared a meal for the sisters and the students, which was both a teaching device and a godsend. Each week, she planned the next week's menu for the sisters, starting from basics and moving on to more advanced subjects as the course progressed.

In the last two sessions, the sisters prepared the meals starting from scratch, under Mary's supervision. After eight weeks, the two sisters were not chefs, but at least they could prepare and serve a satisfactory meal.

Mary's efforts paid off, and the sisters were grateful.

The Navy Yard

Same Name

Back in the days before World War II, the Philadelphia Navy Yard was what you could call "biased." As in many other institutions, the "Old Boys Network" was alive and well in the Yard, and, in this case, the "old boys" were the Masons.

It was practically impossible for anyone not a Mason to get into the upper levels of management and very difficult to get into middle management. There were a few exceptions, but these were very rare and these few were really "tokens." In fact, there were some Catholics who left the Faith, became Masons, and were promoted. I knew a few of them, and they reminded me of St. Thomas More's statement to his young friend, "But for Wales?"[15]

The man who decided who would get what was the Chief Clerk of the Yard, officially. Unofficially, he was the representative of the Masonic Temple, and he had the power. His name was Bert Crowley.

When an officer was assigned to the Yard, the Masons soon determined if he were one of them. If he were, he was inducted into an organization known as the "Sojourners" and worked with the local Masons.

World War II changed all of that, and the Chief Clerk retired during the buildup of the Yard before the War. The expansion was rapid, and, during the War, the management of the Yard passed into the hands of Reserve Officers—many of them Catholics—who could care less about continuing the Masonic stranglehold.

When I became the Labor Relations Superintendent in 1946, there were still a number of people around who remembered Bert Crowley with fondness or with hatred. They, of course, were anxious to see where I fitted in, and the questions to me were sometimes direct and sometimes subtle. Sometimes I was asked, "Are you related to Bert Crowley?" Sometimes, the question was only after a roundabout conversation.

When I told them I never heard of Bert Crowley until I came to

---

[15]From the movie, A Man for All Seasons: "Why Richard, it profits a man nothing to give his soul for the whole world... but for Wales?"

the Yard, those who loved him were disappointed, and those who hated him were relieved and explained in great detail what a son of a bitch he was.

I used to wonder sometimes if Bert "took the soup."[16]

---

[16]During the Irish famines, various religions set up soup kitchens to feed the starving of their own faith. Since the Protestant churches were richer, and Protestants fewer in number, they had more soup to give out. Catholics who changed religions to take advantage of this were said to "take the soup."

Harry's Party

About a month after I went to the Shipyard, my assistant, Sam Kaplan, asked me to go to a retirement party for his former boss, Harry Steiner. I said I would be glad to go.

Harry worked in the District Headquarters for over 45 years and, when he retired, he was a clerical supervisor. He was liked by a great number of people, and his party was well attended.

After the obligatory remarks concerning him and his career, Harry addressed the assemblage, and I still remember what he said. He introduced his wife, thanked everybody for coming, told his co-workers how much he appreciated them and how much he would miss them. Then said that he wanted to tell them what his wife had given him as a retirement present.

After he retired, Harry and his wife were having breakfast one morning when she said it would be a beautiful day for a ride to the Shore. He agreed and reminded her they didn't have a car. She asked him to come out front with him. He did and noticed a brand new Buick parked in front of their house. He wondered whose it was. She handed him the keys and told him it was his. When he recovered from the shock, his wife told him she was ready to drive him to Brigantine.

When they arrived at Brigantine, she drove to a beachfront house, parked and told Harry to come into the house with her. He hung back, saying that they didn't know the people who lived there, and they probably would be thrown out if they went in. She assured him that wouldn't happen, and opened the door with a key. They entered a beautifully furnished home. By this time Harry was completely confused and asked whose house this was. Mrs. Steiner replied, "It's yours!"

Harry then told us how this wife arranged all of this without his knowing a thing about it and publicly thanked her, adding that they both looked forward to spending his retirement together in their beach house.

I was impressed and wondered how a clerical supervisor could afford gifts like these. I guessed that his wife had money.

A year or so later Kaplan asked me if I would contribute to a burial fund for Harry Steiner. I said I would and asked what happened to Harry's' money. Sam said that Harry had no money and never did. I asked about the car and the beach house, and Sam told me there never was a car or a house. In fact there was nothing but Harry's pension, which barely supported him and his wife. When I asked why Harry said what he did at his party, Sam shrugged and said, "That's Harry."

Sam also told me that Harry, dressed in work clothes, went to a neighborhood bar several days a week and told anyone who would listen that he started his men on the job earlier and they didn't need him for a while. About four o'clock, he left the bar, stating that he had to go and check on his men before quitting time. Of course, there were no men and no job, and Harry went home.

I used to wonder why Harry acted like this, but never could come up with a reason.

Commodore John Barry

For many years, the Masons ran the Navy Yard and practically everything else in Philadelphia. The Mason's man on the scene was Bert Crowley (no relation) who held the imposing title of "Chief Clerk." He had the power, and the Masons took care of their own.

I was surprised, when I went there in 1946, to learn that the Master Coppersmith, Archie Allen, was a Catholic and had been a Master since the 1930's. He had made it even in the reign of King Crowley—most unusual.

Over the years, I got to know Archie very well, and he was a fine gentleman. As they say, a credit to our Faith.

He told me a story about his activities when he was a young man. He and a few other Catholics thought John Barry had never been given the recognition he deserved solely because he was a Catholic. There was no statue honoring Barry anywhere, as far as they knew, and they thought it only fitting that there should be a statue of him in his home town. The most appropriate site, they believed, was at Independence Hall.

At that time, City Hall had jurisdiction over the Independence Hall, and the Masons owned City Hall. The first efforts of Archie and his friends met a stone wall, and their suggestion was rejected out of hand. Undaunted, they solicited the aid of other Catholics and eventually built up so much pressure that City Hall couldn't refuse their request.

Archie and his group could have their statue of Barry, but it had to be placed in back of Independence Hall—not in front.

The Hall was at that time in the middle of a business district with a row of buildings facing across Chestnut Street. The back, however, stretched to Walnut Street and had been neglected for years. This was where the statue was to be placed. Later, this area was transformed into a beautiful park. John Barry presides over it, and hundreds of thousands of snapshots show his statue in a beautiful setting.

Archie Allen has long since gone, but the result of his vision and perseverance still looks out to Walnut Street. The Father of the American Navy has a home at last.

(Photo by Jim McWilliams, courtesy of PCVB)

They Wanted Their Report Back

When I was the Legal Counsel and Executive Secretary to the Navy Security Hearing Board, I reviewed thousands of dossiers of reported security risks—some great, some small, some none at all.

I remember receiving a file one day and, when I started to review it, I knew we had something big.

The subject was a welder in the Yard, and he was a busy boy. He was active in every Communist cell in Pennsylvania, New York, and New Jersey; and in most of them he was either the head man or his assistant. I began to wonder where he ever found the time to be a welder, but apparently he had. The evidence against him was overwhelming, and I was convinced that he was the biggest fish I ever ran across.

I spent several days building a case for presentation to the Board and was just about wrapping it up when I got a call from the local office of a federal security agency, asking for an appointment with me as soon as possible. I set it for early that afternoon, and at two o'clock I was told by the Marine at the Gate that two agents were here to see me. I cleared them in, and shortly the two appeared at my office.

After the introduction, they told me that they were here on a matter of utmost security. I said I was cleared for Top Secret and asked to see their clearances. They were cleared for Secret. Then I asked how I could help them.

After some hemming and hawing, they asked me if I held the file on John Doe. I said I did, and then they asked me to give them the file. When I asked why they wanted it, they said they couldn't tell me. I told them they couldn't have it. Then they went out in the hall for a conference.

When they came back, they said they would ask the Shipyard Commander to give them the file. I said, "Fine," and offered to walk them to his Office. They went into the hall for another conference.

When they came back again, they said it was a matter of National Security that they be given the file. I said it was a matter of National Security that I keep it, and, if they had nothing more to discuss, the meeting was over. I got up, and then one of them said,

"Wait a minute, can't we work this out?" I said I didn't know and what did they have in mind.

Finally the spokesman said that what he was going to say was secret and asked me not to repeat any of it. I said I knew more about security than he did, and I understood my duty not to disclose.

Then he told me the story.

The investigation of John Doe uncovered all the facts in the Agency report, and all of them were provable. The one thing the Agency didn't find out in their investigation was that John Doe was an undercover agent of another security agency. If we charged him, it would blow his cover and embarrass both agencies. I told them that they both deserved to be embarrassed for such sloppy work. They said nothing.

I told them I'd think about it and let them know my answer the next day. They protested and I said, "OK. My answer is no, and we are charging John Doe." They panicked and said tomorrow would be fine and left.

Normally, I wouldn't go through this fan dance, but that particular agency was a very uncooperative outfit. They would not let anyone look at their files. They read them to you instead and in general told you as little as possible.

So I let them squirm for a day or so and turned the file back to them with a warning to get their act together. I'm sure they appreciated my advice.

Bargaining with Bankers

When I was working at the Shipyard, I became friendly with a bank representative. Strange as it seemed to me, he was a salesman, and his job was to convince people to borrow money from his bank.

After a while, he asked me how much money I owed, and, when I told him none, he told me I had no credit rating and that wasn't good. I said that Mary and I paid cash for what we bought, and, if we didn't have the money, we didn't buy it. He just shook his head.

A couple of weeks later, he asked me to consider borrowing some money from a bank—he didn't say his—even if I didn't need it, and I said I'd give it a try. He gave me some advice, "Remember that you can bargain with anyone."

Some time later, I decided to take his advice. I went to the Girard Trust Co. and told the Loan Officer I wanted to borrow a thousand dollars. I filled out a form and answered some questions. He left me, came back and said I could have the money at 8% interest.

I told him I wanted to pay only 3%, and he said that was impossible. I thanked him and started to leave. He stopped me and asked me to speak to his boss, the Head Loan Officer. I said, "Sure," and he took me to his superior.

We went through the same routine, and the Head Officer said he couldn't give me a interest rate lower than 8%. I thanked him and started to leave when he asked me to speak with the Vice President. I said, "Sure."

He introduced me to the VP telling him I didn't want to pay more than 3% interest on a thousand dollar loan. The VP said that was impossible and the bank charged its employees 4% percent. I said my credit was as good as theirs and I would pay 4% percent. The VP told me it didn't work that way, and I would have to pay more.

I said I understood and I would pay 5% percent. After some negotiating, we settled on 5.5% percent, and I got the money. We put it in a bank account. Now we had a credit rating..

Years later when I was negotiating contracts and was told that something was non-negotiable, I remembered my experience with the bankers and smiled to myself.

Everything is negotiable under the right circumstances.

Unions

Devil and Imps

Three imps were about to go into the world to recruit people for Hell. It was necessary for them to be successful before they could become devils.

Before they left, Satan met with them and asked each what he would do in the world to recruit new members.

The first imp said that he would try to convince every one he met that there was no God. Satan said, "Good."

The second imp said that he would try to convince every one he met that there was no Hell. Satan said, "Good."

The third imp said he would try to convince every one he met that they had lots of time. Satan said, "That's my boy."

The first imp must have been successful since there are lots of people who believe there is no God.

The second imp must have been successful, too, because lots of people believe there is no Hell.

But it was the third imp who really hit the jackpot because most of us believe we have lots of time.

As a matter of fact, we don't have lots of time. We don't have lots of time to do the things we should do, or to do the things we must do, or to do the things we want to do.

And we certainly don't have lots of time to learn how to manage in the presence of a union.

So let us begin.

The Italian Union Leaders

After Word War II, the Government started a program to acquaint foreign union leaders with unions and government in this country. It was part of my job to greet these people when they visited the Shipyard and show them how unions worked with our government. One day, I was told that an Italian group was coming to the Shipyard in a week and their shepherd and translator would be Jim Toughey, a State Department employee. Toughey was an Irish American who spoke several dialects as well as classic Italian.

I told our newspaper editor of the visit, and was overheard by Vince Faccioli, who happened to be in the office. Vince was a messenger who liked to be in on things. When he heard the Italians were coming, he told me that he would like to be their interpreter. I told him that they were bringing one with them, but he pressured me. I finally told him I'd ask Toughey, and if he approved, Vince was in.

I asked Toughey when the group arrived, and he said Vince could take over for him. At out first meeting, Vince was there raring to go.

Toughey opened the meeting, set out the schedule and introduced me. Finally he introduced Vince and said he would be the interpreter while the group was in the Shipyard.

At that, the Italians—all of them—started talking to Vince, who looked like he was being hit with a two by four and sank deeper in his chair, not saying a word. They were asking him about his family and where he came from in Italy. Vince hadn't the faintest idea of what they were talking about and showed it.

I nodded at Toughey, and he took over. Vince left the room and didn't come to see me until after the Italians had left. He started to explain about different dialects, and I told him I understood, and that he did his best. I didn't tell him his best was awful.

I guess there is Italian and Italian, and never the twain shall meet.

Vince never asked me to let him interpret again, although we had several other groups of Italians visit us.

Many years later a similar thing happened to President Jimmy

Carter. When Carter was visiting Poland he brought his interpreter with him. In his opening remarks, Carter said he was glad to be with the Polish people. The interpreter said Carter wanted to have intercourse with the Polish people. It lost something in the translation.

Them Bells

It seemed that there was a new problem every day at the Shipyard, and it also seemed that I was called upon to solve each one of them.

Take the Cafeteria for example.

The cafeteria opened about 6:30 in the morning to accommodate those workers who didn't have breakfast at home, and it stayed open until nine. One day, I was told that many of our managers complained that some employees in their offices were not at their desks at 8:30—when the work day started—but came in late because they were eating in the Cafeteria. I said that was interesting and asked why they were telling me. They replied that, since I was in charge of discipline in the Yard, they thought I could solve the problem.

I said I didn't know what the problem was since the managers could tell those employees not to linger in the Cafeteria and be at their desks at 8:30. Their spokesman looked at me as if I were an idiot and said I didn't understand. He said that the managers didn't want to tell the employees they were late since that might destroy the supervisor-employee relationship. In other words, the supervisors didn't want to do the unpleasant part of their job.

I asked if the time clock showed the employees clocked in late. They said it didn't since the employees clocked in before they went to the Cafeteria. I suggested they be told to clock in only when they reported to work. Again I got the look and was told they couldn't do that.

What a difference between the way the office workers and the blue collar people were treated!

I said I'd look into it, and they assured me they would appreciate whatever I could do to get their employees to be on time.

A few days later, I went to the Cafeteria about 8:15 and had a cup of coffee. I noticed that a very loud bell rang at exactly 8:30, and all the workers who were in the Cafeteria got up from the tables where they were sitting and left. I went back the next day and noticed the same thing.

I told the Cafeteria Manager, Frank Scott, to ring the bell at 8:25 from here on in. He said he would.

I went to the Cafeteria the next morning and had my coffee. The bell rang promptly at 8:25, the workers got up and left. I noticed the same thing the next day.

I asked the complaining managers if their workers were getting in on time. They said they were now, and they had no complaints. They also had no thanks for me.

I assumed that my solution was the proper one since I never heard of the "problem" again.

Joe Gahagen vs. George Meany

When I was the DCPD[17], one of the people I did business with was Joe Gahagen. Joe was a Field Representative of the AFL-CIO and worked directly for George Meany. These representatives had a lot of freedom to do their job and all had a desire to go to the Washington Headquarters as little as possible.

But it so happened that they were called to Washington frequently for meetings, which they considered a waste of time. As these meetings increased in frequency, they became frustrated. One meeting to which they were called was the straw that broke the camel's back.

When they arrived at the Union headquarters, they found that the meeting was postponed for two days and they were to hang around Washington for the meeting. They pleaded for permission to go home but were refused.

All ten of the representatives stayed in the same hotel, and, one evening after dinner, they decided that the only way to make their voices heard was to form a union.

So they drew up the necessary papers and wrote a letter to George Meany requesting that he recognize their union. When Meany got the letter, he went ballistic. When he settled down, he fired all ten representatives.

After they were fired, the representatives went to the NLRB and asked the Board to file an Unfair Labor Practice charge against Meany and the AFL-CIO.

The request was bucked up to the Chairman, who asked the reps to hold off for a few days till he looked into the situation. They agreed.

The Chairman lost no time in contacting Meany and told him he was in deep trouble and advised him to rehire the reps immediately or face the consequence.

Meany fumed but finally gave in. He had his assistant write to each rep, rehiring him with no loss of pay or benefits. After they received their letters, the chairman of the NLRB contacted them

---

[17]District Civilian Personnel Director

and asked if they wanted to pursue their case. They said they didn't.

They all reported to the headquarters for work, finished the paper work and were told to return to their area and continue to perform their duties.

Meany never again called all the reps to Washington at one time. Each was called individually, and only when necessary, and there were no more group meetings.

The devil has work for idle hands.

Remember Me?

While I was the Labor Relations Superintendent at the Naval Shipyard, I had my share of union people who hated my guts. I also had my share of people who thought I was great—at least for a while. When I received a request from a union official, I looked into it and made a decision. Then I told him what I had decided.

The decision was not always well received. But I would "tell like it was" and remind him that I could lie, and he would think I was the greatest thing since ice cream—until he found out I had lied. Then I would be the biggest bastard he ever met. So I would tell him that if he didn't like my decision, he could think of me as a big bastard right now. And we could move on.

Like the story of the union executive board that wished a labor relations man a speedy recovery by a vote of three to four.

Of all the people I crossed swords with, the one who hated me the most was Fred Goleta, the president of a Veterans Union. In our meetings, if a fellow officer even intimated that I might be right, Fred would threaten to bring him up on charges before the union's disciplinary board. As they say, Fred was a piece of work.

Suddenly Fred stopped coming to see me, and he didn't call either. I was beginning to believe that I had been delivered from that hair shirt when an amazing thing happened.

I received a call from the Gate that a Mrs. Goleta and her two children wanted to see me and preferred not to tell their business to the marine on duty. I cleared them and asked the guard to send them to my office.

Mrs. Goleta arrived with her two children. She was a plain middle-aged woman, and she and her children were near tears. I didn't know what to make of this visit. But she soon clued me in.

It seemed that Mr. Goleta was now confined to Lakeland—a mental institution near where I now live—and sent his wife to ask me for help. I was shocked and asked her if he really wanted my help. She assured me that he did, and I didn't know what to say.

He wanted me to arrange for his wife to receive his checks, and for me to advise her on handling the money she would receive. I told her I would see what I could do and would let her know the next day.

I spoke to the Admiral, who told me to help if it were legal, and to the financial management people, who told me what Mrs. Goleta would have to do. I met with the family the next day and helped them with the paper work. When it was finished, Mrs. Goleta said that her husband would like to see me at Lakeland and pleaded with me to go. I didn't know what to do considering my experience with Goleta.

But I decided to risk it and went to Lakeland. After passing through several locked doors accompanied by an orderly, I met Goleta in his room. He greeted me like a long lost brother and told me how much he appreciated what I had done for him and his family. This was definitely not the Goleta I knew.

He said that his wife never handled the family money and asked me if I would help her. I told him I could not manage his finances and would have nothing to do with the money, but, if his wife needed advice, I'd be glad to help. He said that's all he wanted and again told me how much he appreciated my interest. He then asked if I would visit him about once a week. I said I would try.

I couldn't believe what I was seeing. Here was a man who hated me, yet he was acting as if I were his best friend. I thought, if this is what mental illness does to a man, we all should have it. He was pleasant, friendly and just good company. He didn't act at all like I heard the mentally ill are supposed to, and he had none of the bitterness I saw in the Shipyard.

Over the next three months, I visited him a number of times and advised his wife when she asked me

Then one day I got a call from his wife, who told me Goleta had been released from Lakeland, that he was fully recovered and had asked our disbursing office to send his checks again. I told her how happy I was for them and asked if I could speak to Goleta. She said he was sleeping and she didn't want to disturb him. I said I understood.

I had forgotten all about the episode when one day my assistant told me the Veterans' Union wanted an appointment with me. We set it up for that afternoon, and at two o'clock the union officers led by Mr. Goleta appeared. He started where he had left off several months ago, accusing me of everything he could think of. I couldn't believe it. But it continued for an hour, and I didn't know what to say.

This set the tone for our relationship, and it was just the same as it had always been—bad. I wondered what happened to the nice guy in Lakeland. I much preferred him!

One day at lunch, I told this story to a friend of mine who was a Navy psychiatrist, and he set me straight. He said that Goleta didn't remember one thing I did for him and his family. For him, that whole period didn't exist. He said I shouldn't be surprised; it happens all the time.

In my later meetings with Goleta I often wished that the nice guy from Lakeland was still around.

How High the Moon

If there was one thing the Unions in the Shipyard took a hard line on, it was "jurisdiction." I had many difficult days trying to convince one or the other of them that we were assigning work properly. But even beyond jurisdiction, which was a family affair, the Unions were united in their opposition to "contracting out."

The mere rumor that we might be thinking of having a private contractor do some of our work brought the Metal Trades Council, representing all the Unions that felt threatened, to my office, screaming and promising dire reprisals.

We had a 200-foot radio tower in the Yard, and of course it had an array of warning lights at the top. When a bulb burned out, we hired a steeplejack firm to replace the bulb. We had been doing that for years.

This time when the bulb burned out, we asked a couple of firms for bids, but, before we could make a decision, the newly-elected president of the Electricians' Union informed me that, if we contracted that work out, we would be violating Navy policy and our promise to the Union. I told him we had been doing that for years, and he said, "No more." If we tried it, he'd file a grievance with the Navy Department. He was out to show his members that they made no mistake when they elected him, and now we had an annoyance.

We discussed our problem and some possible solutions and finally decided that the hassle wasn't worth it. We wouldn't contract the work out but instead let our electrician change the bulb. The president was convinced that he had scared us off, and the word passed around quickly throughout the Yard. We told the Master Electrician to assign a qualified electrician to the job and forgot about it. But not for long.

In less than an hour, the Master called us back and said the electrician assigned refused to climb the tower. We told him to assign another qualified man to the job and let it go at that.

In less than an hour, the Master called us back and said the ten qualified men contacted all refused the assignment. Now we had a problem.

I was assured by the Master that all the men who refused were qualified electricians. I told him to address a letter to me detailing the facts. I would prepare Letters of Charges for them and tell them of our intention to dismiss them for failure to follow a legal and legitimate order.

No sooner had the men received my letters, than the president and the other officers of the Union stormed into my office, protesting my actions. I asked them why they were upset. We had done what they wanted, and now they were complaining. I told them the electricians were qualified and that refusal to obey a lawful order called for dismissal in our Table of Penalties, as they well knew.

I reminded them that it was their president who wanted them to change the bulb; that he thought they were qualified to do so; and that he said it was their work. End of discussion. Period.

Then I got the appeal to my better side. I told them that what they were seeing was my better side, and the men would be fired. If they wanted, they could appeal to the Navy Department.

Shortly after the group left, the president came back alone and asked if we couldn't work something out. I asked, "What?" and he said maybe a lesser penalty for the men. I told him he raised a big stink about nothing just so he could look good and I was in no mood to bail him out.

After a great deal of pleading, I told him I would reduce the proposed penalties to Letters of Warning on the basis that the men had been mislead by their president into refusing a proper job assignment. He objected strenuously, and I said, "OK, everything stands the way it is." I finally told him I would not say who mislead the men with this condition—that he stop rabble-rousing, and that he would come to me first if he had any problem. He agreed and thanked me. I reminded him that he might not be so lucky next time, and that I may not be in such a good mood.

We had the steeplejack company do the work; the president came to me with his problems first; the word spread that I saved the president's ass; and we got along fine from then on.

The Electrician

At the Shipyard we tried to be understanding. So when an electrician, Max Golden, suffered a slight stroke, the Shop assigned him to inside work and didn't apply the regular rotation of ship and shop. This rotation was liked by the employees because it gave everyone a chance to get out of the weather and do shop work for a while.

No one complained when Max was taken out of rotation and assigned to the shop on a more or less permanent basis. For a while.

But when eight months went by and the other electricians saw their chances of getting shop work reduced, they started to complain. The problem was given to me.

Max was living with his daughter and her family and was driven to and from work by a friend. Max was entitled to a good pension under disability retirement, and I saw that he really was disabled. What he was doing was made work with no pressure.

When the pressure became too great, Max was brought over to me, and we discussed his retirement on disability. He said that he would like to discuss it with his daughter, and of course we agreed.

A few days later, we met with Max, his daughter, and his son-in-law, and the problem soon became clear to me. Max's family wanted him to keep working because they didn't want him around the house all day. His daughter told me there was nothing wrong with her father, and, to prove her point, she asked him to walk across the room. It was pathetic to see the old man trying to walk without holding on to something. It took two minutes to take four steps with his daughter cheering him on. I said he didn't look able to work to me, but she disagreed and said she would bring me a doctor's statement to the effect that Max was fit to work in the Yard.

We met again the next week, only now Max's doctor attended the session and gave me a statement that Max was fit to work, and that work would be good therapy for him. Max said nothing in these two meetings, either because he couldn't or because he was afraid.

The actions of his daughter, her husband and the doctor made me sick in my stomach. They didn't give a damn about Max—they just didn't want the old man in the house.

I said I accepted the doctor's statement and, beginning tomorrow, Max would be assigned to electrician duties aboard ship. Since the doctor said he was able to perform electrician duties, if Max did not accept or perform these duties I would separate him for refusal to work.

This hit them like a bombshell, and they said I could not do that and that I had to assign Max to the "made work" he had been doing. I said, "Watch me." Then they asked for time to discuss this. I said, "Sure."

After a half hour discussion, they said that Max would apply for a disability separation. I said, "Fine" and that we would help him with the paper work.

I put Max on sick leave until his papers came through, and the old man retired on disability, much to the chagrin of his daughter, who was a real bitch.

Sometimes Too Good is Bad

When I was the Labor Relations Superintendent at the Navy Yard, I started a grievance policy which I thought would improve relations with the Unions and our employees.

Under my policy, we would carefully review every grievance, conduct a thorough investigation, hold a hearing and, if the facts warranted it, we would grant what the grievant asked. All doubts were resolved in favor of the grievant.

If the facts did not warrant granting the request, we would steadfastly refuse the request and let the grievance be appealed to the Navy Department. In other words, we followed the textbook approach to grievance resolution. But we really did it, not just pay it lip service. And we gave the grievant the benefit of any doubt.

As could be expected, we never lost a case on appeal, as far as I can remember. We were proud of our record. In fact, the Navy Department on many occasions complimented me and cited my Grievance Procedure as a model for other Installations.

One day, I was called by a Navy official—a friend of mine—who asked me if I would come down to Washington and see him and some other Navy people. Since I was called to the Navy Department frequently, I said I would be down and didn't think any more about it.

The meeting began on a strange note and was different from my other meetings with this group. They seemed embarrassed, and I couldn't figure why.

Then my friend told me the story.

It seemed that Metal Trades Council—the union coordinating organization—complained to the Secretary of the Navy that their member unions in the Philadelphia Shipyard never won a grievance appeal of any of my decisions. The Council somehow considered this to be an anti-union action on my part and wanted the Navy to do something about.

I knew that the officials who told me this were very familiar with my policy, and, in fact, had complimented me many times in the past on my grievance resolution record. As they talked around Robin Hood's Barn, I saw the light.

The Navy, for many reasons—almost all political, wanted to maintain good relations with unions. The last thing it wanted was for some senator or congressman to accuse it of anti-union activity, and my grievance policy could result in just that.

After an hour or so of praising me and, at the same time, shaking their heads, I asked the officials what they wanted me to do, and I knew exactly what would happen.

The reaction was what I expected. It was about the same as it would have been, if I asked them to march down Pennsylvania Avenue naked. There was hemming and hawing, passing the buck from one to the other, asking me if I understood the situation, complimenting me on a wonderful job, wondering if there was anything I could do to solve the problem, and finally telling me that the Secretary would appreciate and remember my help with this problem. It was a classic exercise in CMA.[18]

I had put the Navy over a barrel, and only I could get them off. The Navy couldn't tell me to change my policy. That would really expose the officials for what they were. The Navy couldn't tell the Council to get lost. That would probably result in a Congressional inquiry inspired by the Council's complaint.

So I said that I understood the problem and would try to find a solution. This brought sighs of relief, and promises of appreciation for anything I could do. I didn't believe any of it.

I wrestled with the problem back home and finally solved it. The Navy was happy, the Secretary was happy, my friends in Washington were happy, the Council and the Unions were happy, and I learned that being too good can be just as bad as being bad, maybe even worse. I also learned again that many people, unlike thieves, are without honor.

---

[18]acronym for "Cover My Ass"

Government

Connally and the Admirals

In the early 1960's, I was in Washington conferring with a friend of mine who was the Director of Civilian Personnel for the Chief of Naval Operations. We hadn't quite finished our business when he told me he had to stand by in case he was needed since John Connally, the Secretary of the Navy, was going to speak at a CNO[19] meeting. He said we could finish our business while he was standing by. We went to the anteroom of the CNO's conference room.

When we got there the meeting was in progress, and we could see all the admirals listening to a speaker.

We had finished our business and were chatting away when a tall, distinguished-looking man came in. When he saw us he came over, held out his hand and said, "John Connally." We introduced ourselves, and he asked us what we did. We told him.

He said he had a lot of experience with civilian personnel when he was the Governor of Texas and proceeded to tell us some of his experiences.

He was in the middle of one story when an admiral saw him, and the speaker quickly put away his charts. The CNO came out of the conference room, and when Connally looked at him, he said, "We're ready for you now, Mr. Secretary." Connally said, "Fine," and continued telling his story to us. The admiral stood there. When he told the punch line—about 5 minutes later—we all chuckled, including the admiral.

Then Connally got up as we did, shook our hands, and told us how much he had enjoyed chatting with us. Then he said to the admiral, "I'm ready now," and went into the conference room.

This is called positioning, and he did it like the pro he was.

I never saw or talked with Connally again, but I remember him.

---

[19]Chief of Naval Operations

The Best Laid Plans

When I first met Larry Bayer, he was about sixty years old.

Larry was the Assistant Director of the New York Civil Service Region and had been for about fifteen years. We worked on a number of projects together since my District and his Region overlapped. I found him to be a smart, capable, and pleasant man, and it was fun to work with him.

He had never been picked for the Director's job, although he had served under five directors. He was a perfect number two man who interpreted the top man's shout into an understandable and workable program. Maybe it was this ability that kept him where he was. I never knew why he was never promoted. He told me several times that he was looking forward to retirement, and that he and his wife were planning to move to Florida.

But events shaping up miles away were to determine his future.

Two years before Larry's scheduled retirement, the Director retired and the Commission started a nation-wide search for his replacement. I asked Larry if he were applying for the job, and he told me he wasn't since he was sure that the Commission wanted a younger man.

In a few months, the Commission picked one of its assistant directors, Jim Ellison from the West Coast, for the job. Since it was such an important one, it was decided that Jim would spend a year in a post-graduate program at Princeton and then be appointed Regional Director. He was definitely in line for greater things, and the Commission was sparing no expense as far as he was concerned.

In the meantime, Larry would be named Acting Director and keep the chair warm till Jim finished at Princeton and was ready to take over. By that time Larry would be sixty five and could retire.

But things were happening elsewhere.

Robert Kennedy was Johnson's Attorney General, and, to put it mildly, they hated each other. Then Bobby ran for Senator from New York with plans to run for President, and this made the relationship between the two even worse.

As it did on a regular basis, the Navy was planning to close a shipyard. From all indications, this time it would be Philadelphia.

No new work was being assigned to the yard; the maintenance funds were being slashed; unfinished work was being reassigned to other yards; and reductions in force were being planned, as was a freeze on hiring. No official announcement was made, but the signs were all there.

Then Bobby Kennedy was elected Senator from New York and things changed. Someone had decided that the Philadelphia yard would be kept open and the New York yard would be closed. All the things that had happened to Philadelphia now happened to New York. We blossomed, and New York withered on the vine.

When the announcement of closing was made, the Commission and the Navy, together with other Federal agencies, started planning to place separated workers in other jobs. I was on the fringes since the Fourth Naval District covered New Jersey. No employees were yet separated, but, as usual, the media claimed that nothing was being done to help them. As a matter of fact, much had been done, and the agencies were getting ready to swing into action when the RIF[20] took place.

All the negative press set off Senator Kennedy, who joined in the criticism and demanded a meeting with the New York Regional Office. Larry invited me to the meeting, although I was not involved. I accepted.

When the meeting opened, Kennedy launched a tirade against the Regional Office of the Commission, claiming it had done nothing to help the workers who would be displaced, and promising a Senatorial investigation.

Larry said nothing during the half hour tirade. When Kennedy was through, Larry said that he was glad Kennedy had taken an interest in this matter, and that, unfortunately, the Senator had not been properly briefed.

He then laid out in detail what the Commission had done and what it planned to do and gave him the a copy of the plan, the time table, and a listing of what had been done to date. Kennedy leafed through it and asked if he and his staff could be alone for a few minutes. We left the room, and a half hour later an aide said that Kennedy would like to see Larry and his group.

He then told Larry he had no idea of what was being done, and, if he had, he would not have asked for the meeting. Larry said he was glad they met since it gave him an opportunity to show the Senator what was being done and to ask for Kennedy's aid in placing the separated workers.

Kennedy congratulated Larry and his staff, and said he would appoint a senior aide to be liaison between himself and Larry. He

---

[20]Reduction In Force

promised to help Larry in any way he could. Later, the Commission people in Washington told Kennedy they were ready to assist in any way, but he told them he wanted to deal only with Larry.

After the meeting, Kennedy called a press conference during which he praised Larry and said that the two of them would be working together to place the workers who would be separated.

Larry's plan gathered steam as more workers were separated, and Kennedy was happy with what Larry was doing.

The layoffs continued. Half way through that exercise, Jim Ellison finished his studies at Princeton and was ready to assume the regional director job. Larry welcomed him with open arms knowing he could retire at last and move to Florida. But the top people in Washington had other ideas. They told Larry and Jim that it would be unwise to appoint Jim at this time and suggested that Larry stay on till the placement job was finished. Jim would work in the Headquarters for the time being.

Jim wasn't happy with that plan, and Larry said he would not go along with it. He was retiring. Period. His bosses could not convince him to stay, saying they would wave the rule requiring retirement at sixty five, but Larry still said no.

Then he received a visit from Senator Kennedy, who asked Larry to stay on as a personal favor. Larry agreed, and Jim went to Washington.

Two years later, the Shipyard was closed. All the workers who could be placed were, and the project was closed. Larry was the star of the show. Kennedy praised him; the top people in Washington called him the ideal manager and gave him an award; the unions called him a great friend of labor; and the displaced workers who got new jobs loved him.

Everyone expected Jim to be named regional director, but he wasn't. The job was advertised, someone else was selected, and Jim was transferred to another regional office as the administrative officer. Only a few knew why, and they weren't talking.

When the new director was installed, Larry finally retired, toured Europe with his wife for a month, and went to live in Florida. Kennedy sent him a nice letter of thanks.

When I said goodbye to Larry, I asked him if he ever thought about what would have happened if his ability had been recognized earlier and he had been appointed regional director. He said he did once or twice but couldn't decide what would have happened.

One would think the Government's top personnel officer would have done better.

It All Depends

For some reason or other, I was always picked to shepherd foreign visitors by the Office of Industrial Relations in Washington.

One of these was the Director of Personnel for the Indian Navy. He had been the Assistant Director when India was a part of the British Empire and was promoted to the top job when his country became independent.

We spent a week together comparing our countries, and he was a very interesting man. We traveled to some of our activities so he could see how we did things, and he told me how it was in India.

I remember one story he told me about passive resistance, which was used widely by the Indians when the British were in control.

A group of Indians would lie in the road when a company of English soldiers in tanks approached them. The demonstrators were ordered to get up, but they ignored the order. They stayed where they were, effectively blocking the column.

The top sergeant would say to the officers, "The blighters won't move. What shall we do with them?" When the efforts of the officers failed, the column retreated to find another way to their destination.

The Indians' technique was very successful until they tried it against the Russians who were marching into a northern province. They would lie in the road as the tanks approached, but this time the tanks ran over them and killed them.

My friend said passive resistance works only against people who have a conscience.

McNamara's Band

When I was the DCPD[21], the Admiral who commanded the Aviation Supply Office was friend of mind, and we worked together on many projects. He was responsible for procurement, storage, and issuing of all hardware required by Naval aviation, and he had under him a number of depots.

In one of our meetings, he told me a story which describes how Mr. McNamara[22] and his crew operated, which the public knew nothing about. And it's not an isolated case. It happens all the time in government.

Before the Vietnam War, McNamara sent a group from his office to inspect the Aviation Supply Office. The group spent several months going over the entire operations and came up with several recommendations. The only recommendation to which the Admiral objected suggested that he reduce the inventory of helicopter rotor blades by 90%. He pointed out that these blades are fragile, break quite frequently and the number presently in inventory was a reasonable one. The inspectors ignored his opinion, and, shortly after the group left, my friend was ordered to reduce the blade inventory by 90%.

As you can imagine, the demand for helicopter rotor blades is very limited, and the blades were sold as scrap for about 10% of their value.

Then came the Vietnam War, and helicopters by the thousands were shipped to the war zone. The terrain in which they operated was sandy, with small rocks, and their blades were chewed up at an alarming rate. The Admiral was then ordered to build the blade inventory immediately. He went back to the people who had bought the blades as scrap and bought back all they had. The price was 10 times what they had paid for them.

When Congress heard of the situation, it wanted to know why there was a shortage of blades in Vietnam. Hearings were held, and my friend was called as a chief witness.

---
[21] District Civilian Personnel Director
[22] former Secretary of Defense

The day before he was to testify, a member of McNamara's staff called on him and told him that under no circumstances was he to mention McNamara's name or to connect him in any way with the reduction in blade inventory. My friend said he would answer any questions truthfully. And he did.

He was not very popular with McNamara and his friends, but they were afraid to do anything to him. This happened more than 30 years ago. Think of how much worse it is today.

Rugged Individuals

Back in the early 1950's, Philadelphia started to plan for the redevelopment of the area just this side of the Ben Franklin Bridge. The area was bounded on the north by Vine Street, on the south by Arch Street, and ran from 5th to Front Streets.

It had various names—Skid Row and the Tenderloin among them. It was a local labor market for unskilled labor, and, every day, farmers from New Jersey and other employers would come there and hire the men they needed to work that day.

It was also home to thousands of unfortunate people (mainly men with just a few women—less than 50) who lived in rooming houses throughout the area. They lived by odd jobs including delivering circulars (which they called "bundling"), by panhandling and by farm work in Jersey.

The City began preliminary planning, hoping to find the answers to such questions as—Where will these people go if the rooming houses are torn down? Should the City build and manage resettlement housing? What should be done for the small merchants? What special arrangements should be made for the handicapped? And what will replace the existing labor market?

An old friend of mine, Randy Wise, was the City Commissioner of Welfare, and he was in charge of the preliminary planning. He told me that he and a few people from his office were conducting a dry run of interviews to find the kinks in the program and asked me if I would like to join them. I accepted gladly.

Early one Saturday morning, Randy picked me up. I was in for a very enlightening day. I had heard that someone said about the inhabitants of Skid Row—"You might find someone there who was richer than you, or smarter than you, or better educated than you, but you won't find anyone who is luckier than you." He knew what he was talking about.

The six of us who were participating in the dry run were given questionnaires developed by Randy's people. There were about a hundred questions designed to find out a lot about the people on Skid Row: background information, family history, work experience, and opinions were among the areas covered. Each person interviewed was given fifty cents, so there was no shortage of takers.

We fanned out in the area, and during the day we each interviewed about thirty people.

I found out that there were no stereotypes. I had thought that I would be talking only to drunks. I was wrong. It was true that most of the inhabitants were alcoholics, but not all. I found that some of the men wanted to live on Skid Row even though they could move from it. I found that some had well-to-do families living in Chestnut Hill and Germantown, but had, and wanted, no contact with them.

I talked with one who had a college degree and some who hadn't reached eighth grade. I found one who had been an executive and some who never held a full time job. There were some who never married and some who had wives and children living in Philadelphia. There were some living there because they couldn't afford to live anywhere else and some who lived there to escape whatever devils from the past were haunting them. There were some who were neat and clean and some who smelled to high heaven. There were some who said they were eighteen and looked twelve, and some who said they were seventy and looked ninety.

Yet, I never heard any sad stories from them, and I never heard them blame someone or something else, and none of them told me of their plans for the future, if they had any. They were realists.

I saw where they lived and where they hung out, and they told me how they lived day by day.

Many said that the first thing they did each morning was to get twenty- five cents and not spend it. This was the price of a night in a cubicle where they could sleep out of the weather with some degree of safety. After that, anything else they could earn or cage was gravy. It could be spent for food, but, in most cases, I gathered it was spent for liquor or wine. Beer was rarely mentioned. They depended on the soup kitchen in the area for a meal, and often for a place to sleep. Their views about meals were interesting. They told me that anyone who went hungry on Skid Row had themselves to blame. They said there was enough food there to feed an army. Sleeping in a shelter was a last resort since they didn't feel safe there. Theft was a big problem. They liked the cubicle.

I saw where they lived. Each cubicle had a bed and a chair and room for nothing else. The door had a padlock on the inside and the walls were seven feet high. A chicken wire barrier stretched from the top of the wall to the ceiling. Many considered the cubicle their permanent home and told me that it was a good safe place. They all spoke highly of the owners of the rooming houses. They didn't call them "flop houses."

One of the questions we asked was this, "Do you think the City should build and manage shelters for the homeless?" Everyone I spoke to said, "No," explaining that bureaucrats couldn't manage anything—citing instances where the officials messed up. They all said that any shelters the City built should be managed by the same people who managed the flop houses now. They wanted nothing to do with politicians and bureaucrats. They were rugged individuals who didn't trust the Government.

That was more than sixty years ago, and time proved them right. Maybe they should be the "focus groups."

When we finished our work, we exchanged views. We all agreed that we had learned a lot and that once the bureaucrats finished their work, these people wouldn't be around. And that's what happened. The buildings came down, the streets were widened, new buildings were erected, parks appeared, and Skid Row—and all who lived there—disappeared. Progress, but not for everyone.

No one knows where the men and women of Skid Row ended up. They scattered throughout the City. Some may have gone back to their families, some surely have died, and some just disappeared. The City built some housing, but, from what I heard, few, if any, of these people moved in. They just didn't trust politicians and bureaucrats. A lesson for us all.

Teaching

The Story of Seymour Gould

I met many weird characters in my teaching career. Right up there among the top three was Seymour Gould.

Seymour was a graduate of the Philadelphia Public School System, and I often wondered how he got out. His reading skills were practically non-existent and were matched only by his writing ability. His math was adequate, particularly if the problem concerned money. But, if his academic achievements left something to be desired, his "street smarts" were impeccable. He was a Ph.D. in that department.

I used to assign a term paper to my management classes that required them to set up a business. They had to plan every stage from financing the startup to dissolution. I made it clear that the successful completion of this project was critical to their passing the course.

I collected the papers a week before the examinations, and told the students they could pick up their papers at my office on the last day of class. A few were quite good, most good, and some pretty sorry.

The paper turned in by Seymour was outstanding. I have rarely seen a paper as good as his.

Seymour was among the last to pick up his paper. With the self-assurance of an honor student, he asked for his paper. Before I gave it to him, I asked if he wrote this paper on his own. Affecting a pose somewhere between sadness and outrage, he asked me if I thought he didn't write it. I assured him I had no such thought. He then asked me what his grade was, and I told him it was a high "A." He said that he believed he deserved that mark considering the time and energy he put into writing the paper. Then he left for class.

A few minutes later as I approached the classroom, I could hear the laughter and, over it, Seymour telling everyone how he put one over on me. When I entered the room, everyone was silent.

I said that I was sure they all had a chance to look at their papers and the grades they earned. Then I told them how their final marks would be determined.

Those students who were given "C's" for their papers, would pass if they turned in a fair examination. Those who got "B's" would get a "B" or better if they turned in an excellent examination. Those who received an "A" for their paper would get an "A" if they turned in a superior examination. I pointed out that the mark each received for the project indicated the level of his or her ability, and anyone who did not reach this level on the examination would fail the course. After all, I said, each of them had shown me how good she or he was, and I would not accept a lesser performance on the examination.

This announcement was greeted by a profound silence bordering on panic. Then from the back of the room, a clear voice said, "So long, Seymour."

Seymour never showed up for the final exam. I gave him an "Incomplete," which described Seymour and his performance. I later changed it to a "Failure" and never saw Seymour again.

My Colleague

I have heard it said that some of my faculty colleagues were not all there, not playing with a full deck, intelligence challenged or just plain nuts. And sometimes I thought they were all of these. And more!

If you didn't look too closely, they appeared to be sane, normal people. It was only by watching what they did that you could see their real selves. And it wasn't a pretty sight.

Take Warren Wiseman, for instance. If you saw him walking down the hall on his way to class, his arms filled with student papers he was going to return, you might say, "Now there's a highly intelligent, well-educated man." And of course you would be wrong. That's understandable because you saw Warren walking—something he did quite well and required absolutely no thought, but you didn't see the real Warren, and that's just as well.

I saw the real Warren when I returned to my office one day and found him explaining to some students why my secretary was not at her desk.

According to Warren, she had been stapling some papers and somehow stapled her thumb to the desk. He heard her scream, ran to her, pulled the staple out, and took her down the street to the hospital emergency room. There a doctor gave her a sedative, cauterized the wound, bandaged her thumb, and told her to go back to the office and rest. Warren escorted her back to the school and saw that the nurse made her comfortable.

When I was assured that she was all right, I asked Warren how she could have driven a staple into her thumb. He told me she was stapling papers "like this" when the staple gun slipped and drove the staple through her thumb. He demonstrated how it happened and drove a staple through his thumb.

Now it was my turn to accompany the walking wounded to the ER where an incredulous doctor gave him a sedative, cauterized the wound, bandaged his thumb, and told him to go back to the office and rest. I escorted him back to the school and turned him over to an equally incredulous nurse.

That was the real Warren. Appearances are deceiving.

Me and an Indian

In the early 1970's, I conducted a Labor Relations Seminar in Dallas for the Labor Department.

Twenty-five managers from several southwestern states attended, and, as usual, I went to lunch with them. One of the managers asked me if I would go to dinner with him, and I agreed. He suggested a restaurant he said was very good, and he was right.

It was a three day Seminar, and the two of us went to lunch and dinner each day—sometimes with other managers, sometimes just the two of us. He was a friendly man from Oklahoma who had been around, and we shared our experiences.

After the final session, we drove in the same limo to the airport. On the way, he asked me if I knew I had been eating with a part Indian for the past few days. I told him I didn't. He then said he would bet that he was the first person with Indian blood I knew. I told him he would lose the bet since one of my daughters-in-law was part Indian.

He didn't reply, and for the rest of the ride said nothing. My comments were ignored, and my questions unanswered.

When we reached the airport, he quickly left the limo, ignored my goodbye and faded into the crowd without saying a word to me. I still don't know what I said to turn this outgoing, friendly cowboy into a sour pain in the ass.

A Shooting at the Top of the River

Back in the 70's I was conducting a Labor Relations Seminar in San Antonio, Texas for the Department of Labor.

We were in a hotel at the top of the San Antonio River which, at that point, was a little stream overgrown by weeds—nothing like the River downtown.

The room we were using was partitioned off from a larger room used for banquets, and, off to one side, was a kitchen used to prepare meals for banquets.

In the middle of the afternoon, I was lecturing on Preparation for Arbitration when we heard two shots and a scream from the kitchen area. I stopped for a moment waiting for another shot, but none came. So I continued the lecture, but I could sense that the participants were just a little bit nervous. I ignored that, and gradually we all settled down.

At the break, there was much discussion about the happening and all kinds of opinions on what the noise was. I went out to the kitchen and was told that a former boy friend of a kitchen helper, upset over the end of the relationship, tried to kill his former girlfriend. He didn't succeed, ran out of the hotel, and was captured a short time later. She was taken to the hospital, treated for a bullet graze in her right arm and released. I told the group what I had learned and went back to work.

They looked apprehensive when they heard any kind of a noise in the hotel, but there was no repetition of the shooting. This incident gave all of us something to talk about when we returned to our homes.

Chinn Ho and I

In the early 70's I conducted two labor relations seminars in Honolulu for managers in the Customs Service. The first one was attended by managers from the islands in the Pacific and the second by those from Alaska.

Mary and I flew out on the Friday before the Monday I was to start and bullied our way to our favorite corner room on the top floor of the Rainbow Tower. The seminars were to be conducted in a conference room of a Federal Building, and I was in contact with the local Customs people to wrap up the details. We were all set by Saturday afternoon.

On Sunday afternoon, the District Manager told me that the seminars were moved to a private office building in downtown Honolulu. He gave me the address and told me someone would be there by seven AM Monday to give me any assistance I would need.

On Monday I got a taxi and was driven to the building, which was in an older, and not the best, part of town. The office I was looking for was on the second floor of an older building, and when I reached the top of the stairs and knocked on the door it was opened by a Chinese man who said my name and introduced himself as Chinn Ho.

He led me to a conference room that he had set up perfectly with all the equipment I needed. He showed me the "breakout" rooms, told me about the coffee and buns for the breaks. He asked me to tell him if I needed anything, and he would get it for me. He thought of everything and had it all ready for me.

We didn't start until 8:30, and we finished our preparation by a little after seven. I asked if we could get a cup of coffee anywhere. He apologized for not having any in the office, saying that his secretary usually made the coffee and she didn't get in till 8:30. I told him I didn't expect coffee in the office but at some place nearby. He said there was a small shop across the street, and we headed there.

We had our coffee, and he insisted on buying, so I proposed that we take turns buying, and that's the way it was. We went back to the office and waited for the managers.

The sessions went well, and at each break Mr. Ho asked me if I had everything I needed and what could he do for me. At the end of each day, he asked me how it was going and what else could he do for me.

I arrived at the office about 7 every morning, but Chinn was there before. After checking the room, we went out for coffee, and we took turns buying.

The seminars went very well, and much of the success was due to Mr. Ho and his attention to detail.

When we parted after the Thursday session, Mr. Ho said that he would be out of the office Friday and wanted to say goodbye to me now. I thanked him for all he had done for me and told him I had never been treated so well. He said he was glad to help. I asked him to tell me the name and address of his supervisor so I could tell his boss how much he had done for me. Chinn looked embarrassed and said that wouldn't necessary. So we parted.

After finishing the seminar on Friday, I thanked Mr. Ho's secretary, who called a taxi for me. As I headed back to the Rainbow Tower, I bought a paper and read it in the cab. On the front page was a headline saying the owner of the Ilikai had sold it to United Airlines, along with a picture of the sellers and buyers. And there in the picture was Mr. Ho, who was identified as the seller.

I had no idea that the man I shared coffee with was the man in the paper.

I wrote him a note thanking him again and congratulating him on the sale of his hotel. He sent me a note and enclosed a magazine outlining his life and achievements.

He was quite a man.

A Police Escort in Detroit

In the 1970's, I was conducting a Labor Relations Seminar for the Customs Service in Detroit, Michigan.

A few of us went out to dinner one evening and took a taxi to the restaurant. We had an excellent meal, and afterward we decided to taxi over to Canada and look around. One of the group—a fellow from Kansas—said he wanted to see some of Detroit so he was going to walk back to the hotel. We parted, we to Canada, he to the hotel.

Before we began our sessions next morning, he said he would like to speak with me and told me a strange story.

He said he was walking down the main street when a police car pulled up beside him. One of the officers got out and asked him where he was going. He replied he was going to the hotel. The officer told him to get in the car. He protested that he had done nothing wrong, but the officer insisted.

He got in the back of the car and was driven to the hotel. Before he got out of the car, the officer told him never to walk on any street in Detroit at night and to go out as little as possible in the day.

He thanked the officer and promised to do just that.

Moral: Detroit is not Kansas.

Me and Melvin Belli

Back in the seventies, I was conducting a Labor Relations seminar for the Custom Service in downtown San Francisco.

At the end of the day, I hailed a taxi to take me to the Drake Hotel. The driver was a young man who, after a few blocks, asked me if I were Melvin Belli. He seemed so excited that I said yes. Then he began to compliment me on my legal prowess and mentioned a number of cases in which Belli distinguished himself. He said he knew I was Belli as soon as I hailed his cab and told me what an honor and privilege it was to drive for me.

By this time, he was so thrilled that I didn't have the heart to tell him I was not Belli.

When I got out at the hotel he said that when he got home, he would tell his wife that Belli was in his cab. She wouldn't believe him at first, but then would be as thrilled as he was. What could I say? I told him it was a pleasure to meet him and gave him an outrageous tip, telling him to buy his wife something. He refused it at first, but I persuaded him to take it. He reluctantly did after saying he should tip me for my riding in his cab.

I never met Belli—he's dead now—but if I ever did, I should have asked him to reimburse me for the tip.

This was not the first time I was taken for someone else. One time in Austria, it was Harold Wilson, England's Prime Minister. Often it is Pat Moynihan, whom I knew a long time ago.

Maybe I'm Zelig.

Mary, the TV Critic

When I was traveling around the country conducting labor relations seminars, Mary usually went with me. While I was working, she filled in her days by going to museums, art galleries, libraries and similar places. Then we would meet for dinner and go sightseeing or shopping.

One day in Los Angeles, she wandered into a television studio where they were auditioning entertainers who were hoping to get on a show. It was an audience participation thing, where the viewers sat in chairs with all kinds of gadgets, pushing one or the other to express their opinions, and then writing a critique which they handed in after the show.

This day a group of five teenagers were performing, and they didn't impress Mary a bit. The last line of her critique read, "These people have no talent at all. I believe that they will never make it and will disappear in a short time. No sane person would give them a second look."

The group happened to be the Jackson Five, and Mary was wrong, but she was right.

The group—particularly Michael—went on to fame and fortune; but no person in his or her right mind would give them a second look.

Retirement Travels

Surprise

It had been long day.

Mary and I were spending a few weeks in England, and Jim brought David, his eldest, from Algeria (where Jim was working at the time) to London to spend a few days with us.

We had a wonderful time in London seeing the sights, eating in Indian and Italian restaurants, and watching David chase pigeons on the Embankment.

When it was time for Jim and David to return to Algeria, we all rode the train to Heathrow and said, "Good bye," as they entered the gate. It was a sad farewell.

It was only about ten in the morning, so we had to decide how to spend the rest of the day. We decided to go back to London, to do some shopping and just look around. We got off the train near Foyles Bookstore where we saw a copy of Joe's book and bought some other books.

We had lunch, and, while roaming around, we saw a planetarium and decided to watch the heavens for a while. The seats were most comfortable, and we both dozed off for a short time. When the show was over, we were back on the street and noticed we were near Madam Tussaud's Wax Museum. We decided to go in since we had never been there before.

It was quite a place. President Kennedy was there in wax as well as great number of other notables, all well done.

As we roamed from room to room, we separated, and the walking was catching up with me. Finally I saw an empty chair and was lucky enough to sit down in it before anyone else took it.

It was a relief just to relax. I settled in, arranged my packages around me, and rested my head on my arm. I was all set.

After about five minutes, an English family—mother, father, son and daughter—approached me, and the mother said, "Oh look at this one. There's no sign on him. I wonder who he is." The rest of the family said they didn't know but he looked lifelike, even to the coloring of his skin.

I didn't move a muscle while they examined me and commented on my appearance. Finally I lifted my head, looked at the family and said, "Hello." The mother screamed, the children ran to the father, and he shouted, "What's going on here?" Then they all hurried away from me.

They spoiled my rest. Other people started coming toward me to see what the fuss was all about. I walked away, pretending nothing had happened. I joined Mary, and we strolled to another exhibit and then to the exit.

We continued our shopping and wondered what the English family was doing.

Follow the Leader in Cork

On the way to France, the ocean liner Norway stopped at Cobh, Ireland for a day. To speed things up, the management hired Irish tenders to ferry the passengers ashore. We joined a group and were prepared to spend the day sightseeing. Then it started to rain—a slow, steady drenching rain.

We hoped to go into Cork, but we couldn't get a taxi, so we decided to spend our time on the dock browsing in the museum and the stores and a restaurant. We met a Irishman who seemed surprised when we told him we had no relatives in Ireland as far as we knew. He said we were the first people of Irish descent he met who had no relatives in Ireland.

After we parted, we bought a coat and some souvenirs in one of the shops, toured the museum, and prepared to return to the ship.

We just missed a tender, but in a few minutes another one pulled up, and we were the first to board. The gangplank went from the dock to the top deck, and the lower deck was for the passengers. When we got to the top deck, the captain came out of the pilot house, and we asked him if we could sit inside rather than struggle to the lower deck. He invited us in. We squeezed into a small space and sat down.

What we didn't realize was that we were the first on board, and all the others were following us. As soon as we were seated, a woman who was following us appeared at the door, looked in and said, "My Gawd, they don't expect all of us to fit in there, do they?"

The captain explained that there were plenty of seats on the lower deck and showed her where the ladder was. After giving us a dirty look, she went down the ladder.

The tender shoved off, and we had an uneventful trip back to the ship in a crowded pilot house with the crew.

A Tale from Trieste

After a miserable, cold, and rainy three days in Venice, Mary and I were anxious to get home. There was only a slight problem. The Italian airline employees were on a one-day strike.

So we boarded a bus in Venice with a heater that heated only the driver and were driven to the airport in Trieste. Through some reasoning known only to the Italians, the employees decided that certain flights would be allowed to operate, and we were told that our flight would be one of them.

We were assisted by an airline employee who took our tickets and returned a short time later stating that we were all set to fly home in two hours. We were happy at this news since the airport was a madhouse, with people screaming and running around all over the place.

We found a place to stand while waiting for our plane when a large bearded Italian approached us and asked us where we were flying to. He looked exactly like Pavarotti.

We told him, and he asked for our tickets. We gave them to him, and, when he read them, he shook his head and said they were no good and he would get us a plane to Rome since no planes were flying to America that day.

By that time Mary had it. She told him that if he was wrong, look out! She then drew her finger across her throat in that time-honored gesture.

Our friend said, "Mama, Mama," gave Mary a big hug, and assured her he would take care of everything.

And he did. He gave us new tickets and put us on the plane to Rome, where we were met and driven to a hotel to spend the night.

The next day, we were driven to the Rome airport and boarded the plane to New York.

I don't know if our savior was just a kindhearted Italian or if Mary's gesture convinced him she was not a lady to be fooled with.

You're in My Seat

Casablanca had many attractions when we visited there in the 70's. One that was not to be missed was the Ocean Cave. It was a short distance from the center of town, right on the Atlantic Ocean.

One morning we boarded a bus, and in a short time we were at the Cave. But we were not alone. At least a dozen buses were there before us, and more were arriving every minute.

So, following our guide, we trooped to the cave and for the next hour or so we enjoyed the most unusual experience. The waves came crashing in and almost filled the cave—but not quite. Then they retreated, and in a few minutes the performance was repeated. The cave was formed by the waves eroding the soft rock, and we were told that the cave expanded every year.

We left the cave and made our way back to the bus. I was just getting settled in my seat when a small, feisty, and irate elderly lady stood over me and said in a combative voice, "You're in my seat."

I said that I believed I was in my seat, but she insisted that I was in her seat and demanded that I get up and give it to her. I saw she was getting more agitated by the moment. Deciding that surrender was the better part of valor, I moved to another seat. Mary had her own window seat and watched this encounter with amusement.

The claimant settled in my seat, muttering about inconsiderate people who took other people's seats.

As soon as the bus started, the lady screamed, "You're kidnapping me! Where are you taking me? Where are my friends?" The bus driver stopped, and several passengers tried to calm the screamer. Finally, she settled down and began to cry.

Then the truth emerged. She had gotten on the wrong bus.

The bus driver then drove slowly around the other buses, and, when the lady recognized some of her friends standing at a bus, she screamed, "There are my friends."

The driver stopped and escorted her to her friends. Their reunion was something to behold.

Incidentally, she never did apologize to me.

A Pride Of Lions

After a delightful day-long safari in the African wilds, we were returning to the landing strip along a dusty road when the left front tire of our Land Rover blew out.

Blowouts can be expected, but this one happened twenty-five feet from a resting pride of lions. Our anxiety increased when one lion raised his head and stared directly at us.

Our guide and our driver hastened to assure us that we were in no danger since the lions had gorged themselves and would not move for hours. Then the guide and driver quickly changed the tire, and we drove off. The sleeping lions didn't move.

We reached the landing strip safely, got on the plane and away we went.

We sometimes wonder what would have happened if the guide and driver were wrong.

This was the closest we ever were—or want to be—to a pride of wild lions.

Me and Kit

In 1993, Mary, Joe, Barb, and myself traveled through the West in a mobile home. It was a great trip.

Among the many places we visited was Taos, New Mexico, a delightful little town known as an artist colony. We visited a very old church, saw a wedding rehearsal and roamed through the church garden. Very impressive.

The next day, we walked around the town, did a little shopping, bought a few books, and eventually came to Kit Carson's house, now "The Kit Carson Museum."

Kit was quite a character. When he was alive, he saw a piece of ground in New Mexico, and he wanted it very badly. He had the money to pay for it, but there was just one problem. At that time, New Mexico was a part of Mexico, and Mexican law was very clear and specific that only Catholics could buy and hold land. Kit was not a Catholic. But he was resourceful.

If only Catholics could buy and hold land, Kit would become a Catholic. It was as simple as that.

So Kit went to a padre, said he wanted to become a Catholic and he wanted to become one right now. The padre baptized him and welcomed him into the Church. Kit asked for a Baptismal Certificate and was given one.

Armed with the Certificate, Kit went to the Mexican Land Office, presented his certificate, bought the land he wanted and built his house on it. There were no church envelopes in those days (or any record of church attendance), so it's impossible to say if Kit was a practicing Catholic. But he did follow the letter of the law.

We went into Kit's house, and two ladies greeted us. At the table were two signs. One said that the proceeds from the admission fees would go to the local Masonic Lodge. The other said the fee was three dollars a person and children were free.

I handed one lady six dollars telling her it was for Mary and myself. Then I said that Joe and Barb were our children, and, as such, they should be admitted free. The lady hemmed and hawed and told me that they didn't mean older children could be admitted free. I told her the sign was very clear, and, if they meant only young children, they should have said so. Finally, she gave up, and Joe and Barb paid nothing, much to their embarrassment and the ladies' distress.

I think Kit would have been proud of me.

Earthquakes And Us

In all our travels, Mary and I have been in only two earthquakes. The first one was in Lima, Peru and the second in Morgan Hill, California. And, may I add that two are quite enough.

We arrived in Lima on our tour of South America and had just settled in at the Sheraton Hotel. It is a beautiful hotel with a large atrium. We had a room on the 21st floor with a panoramic view of the city and a frightening view down the atrium to the first floor.

After we unpacked, we went to the lobby and listened to a very talented student musical group. Each member wore a medieval costume with flowing scarves—the kind we had often seen in Spain. When the concert was over, we went into the dining room, were seated and reading the menu when we heard a rumble from deep down in the earth. It was a scary sound, and it grew in volume as we looked at each other. It sounded like a dozen 747's taking off beneath our feet.

Our waiter announced in a loud voice that we all were to stay where we were and immediately ran out of the room. We never saw him again.

The rumbling continued for what seemed like an hour—it was only several seconds. The room and the building started to shake, and the ceiling fixtures swayed.

When it was over, everyone in the room looked at each other and started to talk. The conversation became loud—but not as loud as the earthquake—and soon subsided.

A new waiter came to our table, told us everything was fine and asked if we were ready to order. We were, and we did and enjoyed an excellent meal. Of course, the earthquake was the only topic of conversation in the dining room. Strangers talked with strangers, as they never would have in an ordinary situation.

When we went to our room, the maid was there. She told us that she was in the room when the quake hit, and the whole floor swayed. A chair was overturned, some things were thrown off the bureau, and some glasses were broken in the bathroom.

As far as we knew, no one was hurt, and soon hotel life returned to normal. We went to bed and had a good night's sleep.

The next morning we toured the city, and we didn't see any signs of damage from the quake.

Our second earthquake occurred in Morgan Hill, California in 1989.

We had just returned from a trip to Southeast Asia and flew to San Francisco from Hong Kong. We had asked Joe to reserve a room for us near the airport since we planned to fly out the day after we arrived. We called him when we were ready to leave the airport, and he told us he couldn't get us a room. He suggested we get a car and drive down to Morgan Hill.

The World Series was being played in San Francisco, and every hotel and motel for miles around was sold out.

We picked up a car and drove to Morgan Hill, arriving there about four o'clock. After we settled in, everyone relaxed.

It was a balmy autumn day. Joe was out walking; Mary, Barb and Joey were on the patio, and I was taking a nap in a bedroom. Suddenly, I heard the same kind of a rumble that I had heard in Lima. The house started to shake, the noise increased, a lamp fell off the table, and suddenly I was on the floor.

Fortunately, neither the house nor we suffered any real damage, although some nearby places were hard hit. Neighbors came out looking dazed and Mary and Joey helped a woman across the street who was in a fog. Joe told us later that he saw a wave of earth coming down the mountain as he came up the hill from his walk.

Everyone was waiting for the aftershocks, but they were not strong. We spent the rest of the evening on the patio and had our dinner al fresco. Then we went to bed.

We left Morgan Hill early the next morning, hoping to get our scheduled—or another flight—to Philadelphia. The ride to the Airport was the best we ever had. There was practically no traffic, and we made the run in record time. As we neared the airport, we saw cots and tents in the parking lots of the hotels with people still milling around.

Apparently, no one was allowed to stay in the hotels. We heard that many guests partied outside all night with the hotels supplying the liquor.

The airport was pretty much of a mess. Cots were scattered around where they had been all night accommodating the travelers.

We were lucky. Our scheduled flight had been canceled, but we were put on another flight. It was the first flight out of San Francisco after the quake. It was a full flight, and most of the passengers were baseball fans who had flown out the day before to see the game. Now they were on their way home, not having seen the game and having spent the night in a parking lot.

When we were airborne, the captain announced that he had

flown in just as the quake started. He described his approach and his confusion during his descent—checking his instruments and not realizing that he was landing during a quake.

It was an uneventful flight home, and we had another earthquake behind us.

Months later, we went back to Morgan Hill.

San Francisco suffered greatly, but, after several months, it was hard to tell that there had been a quake here at all. Rebuilding was fast. That wasn't true in some other areas.

We rode over the mountains to Santa Cruz and saw the damage caused by the quake. Houses in the country were destroyed; in the towns, buildings were shattered, and people were living in tents. Santa Cruz was hard hit downtown. The street that we so often walked was closed off, with buildings in ruins and condemned.

Logos—our favorite bookstore—was a shambles, and the owners had moved to another location.

All of this, six months after the quake.

Epilogue: Times Change

(A Note to Our Grandchildren)

Mary and I often look back and remember how it was when we were married and what it's like today.

We were married in the Thirties—in the middle of the Great Depression. Back then, when a young couple announced their engagement, the question most frequently asked was—"Does he have a job?"

Today when a young couple announce their engagement, the question most frequently asked is this—"Does SHE have a job?"

Then, too, babies seem to come much later today than they did in the Thirties.

Back then, if a young married couple didn't have a baby after eighteen months of marriage, people said, "I wonder what's the matter?"

Today, if a young married couple has a baby before eighteen months of marriage, people say, "I wonder what's the matter?"

And then there are the "living arrangements."

In the Thirties, just before a young couple was married, they rented a house or apartment—if they were lucky, fixed it up, and moved in when they returned from the honeymoon.

Today, it seems that there are many more options for young people.

We're certainly no experts in this area. In fact we know so little about it that I shouldn't be writing about it at all.

In this area, we follow a modified Clinton Doctrine as far as all the young people we know are concerned. We don't ask, and they don't tell. We have learned that "where ignorance is bliss, 'tis folly to be wise."

Now, if all of this seems to be pejorative or judgmental, we don't mean it to be so. As the day of our particular judgment nears, we try very hard to follow the biblical precept, "Judge not, lest ye be judged."

Not that we always succeed. Since we have an opinion about everything, sometimes we can't resist the temptation to give the

World the benefit of our thinking.

But we try very hard not to judge, and maybe that's the most important thing.

In addition to looking back, we also look ahead.

What a world of wonders await you great-grandchildren! Remembering the inventions and developments that have taken place in our lifetime is awesome.

For example take radio. When I was about 10 years old I built my first crystal radio set on a breadboard. Getting a thin wire—called a "cat's whisker"—on the right spot on a quartz crystal would bring a radio broadcast through a headset. Putting the headset in a glass bowl would let several people hear.

Then came coils and tuners and commercial sets until today we can hear broadcasts from around the world through a radio you can hold in the palm of your hand.

And then there is television. Mary and I saw our first TV broadcast in Macy's store in New York while we were on our honeymoon. The Fordham football team practice was being broadcast from Yonkers to Manhattan. Now we can see broadcasts from around the world.

Or take computers. I saw my first computer in a Navy Design Installation in the late forties. It was being used to determine the optimum placement of fins on torpedoes. The co-inventor, Mr. Eckert, tried to explain it to me, but all I could see were thousands of vacuum tubes in a very big, hot room. Now our laptops are thousands of times more powerful, and we can communicate with the world.

If this all happened in our lifetime, what does the future hold?

Discoveries in Medicine, in Science, in Communications that, even today, are hard to imagine are just around the corner. Today the cell phone, the computer, gene splicing and other inventions amaze us. Even our theories about the Universe are being challenged. We now find that the Earth is not the shape we thought it was, but is pear-shaped. What happens to a well-rounded man in a pear-shaped world?

While the future will bring you all these marvels, it will also bring temptations and challenges that our generation never dreamed of.

Challenges to your values; challenges to your virtues; challenges to your way of life; challenges to your principles; and challenges to your faith. But Mary and I are sure that, with your background and upbringing, you will resist the temptations and overcome these challenges.

So, be good and have fun.

www.ingramcontent.com/pod-product-compliance
Lightning Source LLC
Chambersburg PA
CBHW021003090426
42738CB00007B/638